PAUL
FOR TODAY'S CHURCH

A Commentary on First Corinthians

STANLEY B. MARROW

FOREWORD BY
Thomas D. Stegman, SJ

PAULIST PRESS
New York / Mahwah, NJ

Cover image by Kevin Tietz / Shutterstock.com
Cover and book design by Lynn Else

Library of Congress Cataloging-in-Publication Data

Marrow, Stanley B.
    Paul for today's church : a commentary on First Corinthians / Stanley B. Marrow.
      pages cm
    Includes bibliographical references.
    ISBN 978-0-8091-4855-4 (alk. paper) — ISBN 978-1-58768-329-9
    1. Bible. Corinthians, 1st—Commentaries. I. Title.
    BS2675.53.M37 2013
    227´.2077—dc23

                                                                    2013012625

ISBN: 978-0-8091-4855-4 (paperback)
ISBN: 978-1-58768-329-9 (e-book)

Published by Paulist Press
997 Macarthur Boulevard
Mahwah, New Jersey 07430

www.paulistpress.com

Printed and bound in the
United States of America

CONTENTS

FOREWORD

Saint Paul famously wrote to the Corinthians, "I have become all things to all people" (1 Cor 9:22). Although Stanley B. Marrow, SJ (1931–2012) did not become *all* things to me, he did become many—teacher; colleague and mentor; and, best of all, friend.

Stanley was a tour de force as a teacher. One gift he possessed that Paul did not was eloquence in speech. As his students will attest, Stanley had a way with words. More important than his eloquence was his message. Stanley clearly conveyed God's love that was manifested in Jesus's cross; moreover, he taught that true freedom is expressed in loving, selfless service. In short, he taught what Paul wrote. And Stanley did so not just with words but through the ways he poured himself into preparing for class, grading papers, giving advice, helping souls (compare 2 Cor 4:5). I am forever grateful to him for one of his famous asides: "If you can't make the gospel comprehensible to children, it's probably because you don't understand it yourself." His exegesis assignments were among the most difficult papers I wrote in thirteen years of graduate studies. Stanley demanded clarity and precision. He had no patience for a student's prolixity.

In time, Stanley became a gracious colleague to me. In 2003 I was missioned to teach New Testament at Weston Jesuit School of Theology, in Cambridge, Massachusetts. Although Stanley was not yet ready to stop teaching, the school hired me with an eye toward his retirement. Notice that I do *not* say that I was brought on to replace him. No one could replace Stanley Marrow! Indeed, we worked together for five years. For many people this could have been an awkward situation. But not with Stanley, who was unfailing in his help and support. He did not cling to his "bread-and-butter" classes. Instead, he allowed me to develop courses he had traditionally taught, including one on First Corinthians. He shared with me several resources and bibliographic gems he had collected over the years. He generously offered his critical eye and sharp mind—and he could be very critical (read "tough love")—to some of my early research and writing.

Over the years, Stanley became a great friend. I will forever cherish the Friday evenings when we would go out to eat. He had his favorite eating establishments, ones that could serve up a juicy steak and a Manhattan, straight up. In those times and places he regaled me with stories about his life—his upbringing in Baghdad, the joys and travails of the long course of studies, the wonderful and brilliant people with whom he had rubbed shoulders in the biblical guild. Stanley was in complete agreement with Cicero's assessment of friendship: God gives to human beings, with the exception of wisdom, no greater gift (*De Amicitia*, 6). And the mark of true friendship is sharing all things.

One of the things Stanley shared with me is the manuscript you are about to read. He tried hard to find a publisher in the months before his death, but to no avail. Near the end, he left me a hard copy and disk of this work. I promised him I would pursue its publication. The final thing Stanley shared, a couple of days before he passed away, was a simple request: "Please pray for me." His words revealed, in a touching way, his humble yet sure sense of belonging to the Body of Christ, to the assembly of saints and sinners that the church in Corinth so readily manifested. And it was Paul's first (canonical) letter to that church that Stanley loved so much to teach. The following pages are the distillation of many years of his study, reflection, and dare I say, prayer over this epistle.

I am most thankful to Paulist Press—and, in particular, to Father Mark-David Janus, CSP, and to Dr. Enrique Aguilar—for agreeing to look at the manuscript and, even more, for deciding to publish it. A word of gratitude is also in order to Father Richard J. Clifford, SJ—a longtime colleague of Stanley's—for his wise counsel in the process of editing this work. Readers, I am confident, will also be grateful. Working their way through this text, they will experience what so many of Stanley Marrow's students did: his passion and love for the living word of God that continues to empower, challenge, and give life to those with ears to hear.

Thomas D. Stegman, SJ
Boston College School of Theology and Ministry
Easter 2013

PREFACE

There are innumerable, excellent commentaries on Paul's First Letter to the Corinthians. This book is not one of them. There are very many first-rate studies of this epistle. This work does not aspire to be of their number. This book is rather the outcome of an "insight" that struck me when first I taught this important letter of Paul's. It dawned upon me then, and the conviction grew with the years, that there is scarcely a problem in today's church that is not, somehow, broached by this epistle. To be sure, First Corinthians does not deal with nuclear fission or in vitro fertilization; nor is it expected to. What it does is face the problems the community of believers inevitably runs into as they live out their faith in Jesus Christ.

The late Muriel Spark's guideline for writers was to write as to an acquaintance, a friend, and not—as common wisdom has it—about "what you know." My own attempt throughout was to write to those with whom I share their faith in Jesus Christ. In other words, whoever deigns to read these pages could be counted among those Christians of whom Minutius Felix (second/third century) said, "They love one another almost before they know one another."

Stanley B. Marrow
Easter 2009

Chapter 1

FIRST CORINTHIANS 1

1:1 Paul, called by the will of God to be an apostle of Christ Jesus,…
This first sentence is not only an identification of the sender but also the true warrant of his identity. The Corinthians already know who Paul is, but they need a reminder of the true source of his ministry as an apostle. To be sure, Paul himself is an apostle; a short while before this letter was written, he had brought to them the gospel, the good news of Jesus Christ, but especially because his mission and ministry had, and continue to have, their source in God. His conduct toward them, his labors on their behalf, indeed his whole life, is one uninterrupted response to God's call.

The realization of God's call as the genuine source and ultimate reason of Paul's activity is the basis of his untrammeled liberty in dealing with the community of believers, instructing, counseling, consoling, and directing their steps in the path of peace. His liberty rids him of fear, overcomes his hesitations, spares him the compromises and the tampering with the truth he must proclaim. Awareness that his call has its true source in God and not in man or in any human institution is, ultimately, the reason for his unhindered boldness in preaching the good news and expounding its implications and consequences for the believers.

and our brother Sosthenes. The sentence continues with a needed reminder that collaborative ministry was not invented in our more enlightened times. Other Pauline letters bear witness to this: 2 Corinthians, Philippians, and Philemon are "from Paul and Timothy"; 1 and 2 Thessalonians are from "Paul, Silvanus, and Timothy." Apart from all the evident advantages of such collaboration in the work of the ministry, the fathers of the church were not slow to note that it also served the purpose of charity. The love and respect of the ministers for one another was no less a proclamation of the gospel than the enunciation of its good news.

1:2 To the church of God... Here again the church's very being is attributable to God. It is his "call" (the word whence *ekklesia*, the Greek vocable for "church," is derived) that brings it into existence, and not a plebiscite, or a free association of goodwill partners. In Paul's estimate, the church, whether it be a "house church" ("Aquila and Prisca, together with the church in their house" in 1 Cor 16:19b), a regional church ("at Corinth" in 1 Cor 1:2), or the church at large ("All the churches of Christ" in Rom 16:16), is always "the church of God." Christians ought not allow the all-too-human limits of the church to obscure the presence of God. God's commitment in Christ makes the church "the perfect place for imperfect people."

which is at Corinth,... Corinth is located on the narrow (6 km or 3.7 miles at its narrowest) isthmus between the Aegean and the Adriatic Seas. The geography of Corinth determined its historical and cultural importance. Crossing that narrow isthmus from one sea to the other gave navigators access to the Italian peninsula. From the earliest times, the mighty and the famous dreamt of a canal across the isthmus, but they had to wait for French ingenuity in the nineteenth century to see the dream realized. The ancients, however, were not unresourceful. In lieu of a canal, they devised an overland track, a portage road (the *diolkos*), on which the ships were hoisted at one end, trundled across, and dropped back into the sea at the other. This obviated the lengthy and hazardous sea voyage around the mainland, a voyage that was possible only between March and November, when the weather made those waters safer for navigation.

The historical importance of the site derived both from the varied fortunes of a city "half as old as time," and from the Isthmian games, which, like the famous Olympic games, the Delphic games at the sanctuary of Apollo at Delphi, and the Nemean games at the sanctuary of Zeus in Argolis, where Hercules tackled the Nemean lion, were held at regular annual intervals. It is quite likely that Paul first came to Corinth, perhaps around AD 50, when the city was teeming with people from every imaginable walk of life: poets and orators, philosophers and healers, soldiers and athletes, prostitutes and pickpockets, charlatans and prestidigitators. Rich and poor, mighty and lowly, Jews and Greeks, from every part of the Hellenistic world, constituted the potential hearers of the gospel message Paul brought to that celebrated metropolis in the first dawning of the Christian era.

Not the least of its attractions, however, was Corinth's mythological past and its mottled historical fortunes. It was utterly destroyed by the Romans in 146 BC. Antipater of Sidon, around 130 BC, lamented its passing:

> Where is thy celebrated beauty, Doric Corinth? Where are the battlements of thy towers and thy ancient possessions? Where are the temples of the immortals, the houses and the matrons of the town of Sisyphus, and her myriads of people? Not even a trace is left of thee, most unhappy of towns, but was seized on and devoured everything. We alone, the Nereids, Ocean's daughters, remain inviolate and lament, like halcyons, thy sorrows.

The allusions here would not have been missed by Antipater's contemporaries, as they are, alas, today. But, even today, for a city to claim Sisyphus for one of its kings is no mean title to glory.

But that city was rebuilt and resettled with Italian freedmen (note the mixture of Greek and Roman names in the epistle) by Julius Caesar in 44 BC. This is the Corinth that Paul knew.

to those sanctified in Christ Jesus,... This phrase is applicable to all the believers, then as now. Their sanctification is not the result of their pious devotions and ascetic practices but is solely the necessary outcome of belonging, and belonging exclusively, to Christ

3

Jesus. Anyone who forgets this in trying to interpret a single phrase or syllable of First Corinthians is bound to miss the meaning of the whole epistle. Most of the stubborn objections to this or that aspect of Paul's teaching are attributable to overlooking this one fact: the people Paul addresses are "sanctified in Christ Jesus." Should this be missed by anyone, he goes on to add:

called to be saints... Sanctification describes not only their static condition but their dynamic vocation. The "call" to sanctity, like that of Paul's to apostleship, and the call of the church itself, is the effective imperative of the will of God. Paul's exhortation throughout the epistle, affecting every walk of life, is but explicitation of this call to all the believers "to be saints." One of the most lamentable misconceptions of Christians through the ages is the removal of this category of sanctity from the daily life of believers and the restriction of "saint" to the relatively few individuals who have been officially canonized.

together with all those who in every place call on the name of our Lord Jesus Christ, both their Lord and ours:... This extends the ambit of the epistle to all subsequent generations and to us here and now. What brings us all together is our "call," both the passive being called and our active call on the name of the one Lord, in Corinth, as in Rome, Paris, New York, London, or wherever.

This is an appropriate juncture at which to recall that these pages are written with the conviction that Paul's words to us today are no less cogent and valid than they were to that port city on the Isthmus of Corinth. Their cogency, moreover, derives from the fact that the problems faced by the Corinthian church make up, as it were, quite a thorough elenchus of the problems faced in today's church. Those who plead antiquity and the passage of time forget how unalterable human nature is. We have not invented a single new sin, a modern novelist once remarked. First Corinthians could well serve as a palmary instance of Qohelet's "There is nothing new under the sun" (Eccl 1:9).

1:3 Grace to you and peace from God our Father and the Lord Jesus Christ. This is a usual enough opening salutation in a Pauline letter. It has been often remarked that the formula combines the Greek epistolary greeting *charis*, rendered here as "grace," and the Hebrew *shalom*, "peace." Be that as it may, the combination seems to be peculiarly Pauline, and its meaning is to be sought principally in the gospel that Paul proclaimed. The grace is the gift of God in Christ Jesus, just as the peace is that which is uniquely Christ's gift to all who believe.

The source of this grace and peace is clearly God the Father and the Lord Jesus Christ. That such a formula is in use by the middle of the first century, barely twenty-five years after the crucifixion, is cause for wonderment. The linkage of Jesus Christ with God our Father in such a formula was the stuff out of which was spun the fabric of the trinitarian formulae in succeeding generations.

1:4 I give thanks to [my] God always for you... Thus begins what is called the thanksgiving segment of the epistle. This was common enough practice, and it can be found in all the letters of Paul save Galatians, where Paul's anger makes him skip over the ordinary gestures of civility. The formula of thanksgiving here in First Corinthians is instructive. Paul acknowledges what is so often overlooked in the ministry, namely that those to whom he ministers are God's gift to him, not his to God. Such recognition in any age is bound to make the ministry less exploitative and far less susceptible of statistical mensuration.

because of the grace of God which was given you in Christ Jesus,... Grace, of course, is always the gift of God. In Paul, it signifies not only the superlative gift of the Christ event, that is, the death and resurrection, but also its appropriation by the believer. This is a freely given gift, as all true gifts must be (Rom 11:6). But it has to be just as freely accepted also, else it would be no gift at all. Before this statement gives rise to those endless debates on grace and free will down the ages, however, it must be kept in mind that the believer, in freely accepting the gift of God, realizes simultaneously that the very acceptance is no less a gift.

That the grace of God is given us "in Christ Jesus" is but a paraphrase of Paul's gospel. Christ Jesus is God's gift to us. His death and resurrection constitute the heart of the creed we profess (1 Cor 15:3–5; Rom 1:3–6).

1:5–6 that in every way you were enriched in him with all speech and all knowledge—even as the testimony to [of] Christ was confirmed among you—... God's gift in Christ always has a perceptible, even if at times minimal, external overflow. For the Corinthians, as for us today (Alexis de Tocqueville lamented the "incessant chatter of our loquacious society"), the gift of speech is no less prized, for all our abuse of it. So, too, is knowledge. Yet, gift though it is, knowledge still has to be diligently cultivated, because no gift can exempt us from the onus of nurturing and developing it. Indeed, today's reluctance to assume this responsibility and our impatience to acquire knowledge overnight is so great that it has beguiled us into substituting information for knowledge.

1:7 so that you are not lacking in any spiritual gift, as you wait for the revealing of our Lord Jesus Christ;... Note that speech and knowledge are here recognized for what they are, "spiritual gifts." They belong to the realm of the Spirit because they are part of the grace of God. Like all the gifts of grace, however, they are given for the interim period. For all of us, whether in the first or the twenty-first century, must await "the revealing of our Lord Jesus Christ." Paul firmly believed such an event would occur in his own lifetime (1 Thess 4:17; 5:10; 1 Cor 7:29). It was not his only error, and he shared it with many in the first generation of Christians. What is certain, however, is the fact that all believers, in every age, live in the period of time between, as the Creed puts it, "he ascended into heaven" and "he will come again in glory." Although contemporary Christians are by and large indifferent to this given of the faith, they still need to be continually reminded

6

of it, because it lends urgency to their faith and provides an object to their hope.

1:8 *who will sustain you to the end, guiltless in the day of our Lord Jesus Christ.* This is all the more important to keep in mind because, when the faithful are reminded of the "day of our Lord Jesus Christ," it more often than not scares them out of their wits. Yet, far from generating frenetic anxiety or accentuating the dread of judgment, this is the assurance to which every believer must cling unto the very end. Sustaining ourselves "guiltless" to the end is not our task to achieve, but God's. It is the grace of God that is the subject of these opening verses of First Corinthians (1:4–9). They ought to rid us of all the dread that is self-generated or imparted by deficient religious education. That God will sustain us guiltless to the very end sets us free to live to the full the grace of God given us in order that we will not waste our days repining the past or dreading the future.

1:9 *God is faithful, by whom you were called into the fellowship of his Son, Jesus Christ our Lord.* The surest guarantee and the most reliable proof of being sustained "guiltless" in the day of the Lord is God's fidelity to his promise. His gifts are ever "irrevocable" (Rom 11:29), and it is not for any human being or any institution to revoke the promise or set limits to its efficacy. Christian institutions and their administrators can at times give the impression that they are the granters of God's grace. They are not.

The Corinthians Paul addresses were "called to be saints," "were sanctified" (1:2), were given the grace of God in Jesus Christ (1:4). These gifts are not subject to arbitration. Their loss is contingent uniquely and solely on the individual's rejection of them. Anyone so "called" is, in fact, called "into the fellowship" of God's Son, a fellowship that will receive its crowning significance in Paul's theologizing on the Eucharist in 1 Corinthians 10.

1:10 *I appeal to you, brethren, by the name of our Lord Jesus Christ,...* So begins the main body of the letter. Its opening formula, "I appeal" (from which verb in Greek we have "Paraclete") is the hallmark of Christian preaching and exhortation (1 Cor 4:16; 14:3, 31; 16:16; 2 Cor 1:3–4; and so on). The appeal is solemnized "in the name of our Lord Jesus Christ." The repetition of this title in the opening verses of this epistle is nothing short of astonishing (1:1, 2, 3, 4, 7, 8, 9, and 10). Commentators have remarked that, under the pen of Paul, "Christ" became a proper name: "Jesus Christ." But the insistence on the Lordship of Jesus is significant for another reason. It is a repeated reminder of the subjection and obedience due this Lord. You can believe in God without acknowledging his dominion or sovereignty (Rom 1:21), but you cannot believe in Jesus Christ without submitting to his Lordship. The response to Paul's gospel can only be the confession of Jesus Christ as Lord (Rom 10:9).

that all of you agree and that there be no dissensions among you,... This is the first problem Paul addresses. Report of such "dissensions" must have reached him by word of mouth (1:11); and, aware of their corrosive effects in the community of believers, Paul hastens to address the matter, not with the contemporary platitudes about healthy debate and plurality of opinion, but with a genuine and sincere plea that "all of you agree and that there be no dissensions among you." This is something that is not resolved by fiat but by appeal and admonition. It can be overcome only if those involved come to their senses and comprehend what the "fellowship of his Son," to which they were called (1:9), involves. This is what the confession of Jesus Christ as Lord really means.

Paul's appeal is for agreement among the members of the community. Such agreement is further explained by the absence of "dissension" (the Greek term here is *schisma*). Nothing is more inimical to the fellowship of his Son. Such fragmentation within the community is the unfailing manifestation of the rejection of the Lordship of Jesus Christ. Today's Christians will do well to keep this in mind. The messengers of the word should never forget the need to foster the unity that Christ desires in the church.

To be of the same mind and the same judgment is certainly not an invitation to drab monotony, but a summons to "have this mind among yourselves, which is yours in Christ Jesus" (Phil 2:5). The true source of the unity of mind and judgment in the community is Christ Jesus. Paul's jealousy to safeguard it is not an exercise in totalitarian mind control, but manifest loyalty to the Lordship of Christ in every member of his fellowship. Note that the Philippians text says that this mind is already "yours in Christ Jesus." It is not so much the vigilance of those at the top as the noblesse oblige of the believers that will preserve it.

but that you be united in the same mind and the same judgment. This clause makes explicit what shunning dissensions in the community requires. It does not require uniformity of opinion, nor identity in sentiment. Paul's plea is rather for the recognition and acknowledgment of that which is at the basis of their fellowship and at the source of their call. He is not so foolish as to imagine that obedience to the Lordship of Jesus Christ manufactures clones.

1:11 For it has been reported to me by Chloe's people... Commentaries always hasten to identify the individuals named. This is the only mention of Chloe in the New Testament. The meaning of the text will not be altered one whit if the name were Flora, or Joanna, or what have you. But, in many other cases, a name happens to occur in another context as, for example, the Sosthenes of 1:1 earlier. It occurs in Acts 18:17 as the name of that hapless "ruler of the synagogue" who received a sound beating at the hand of his fellow Jews. The common enough presumption is that the two are one and the same. But such presupposition is untenable. It presumes that only one person could have borne that name, which is of course nonsense in the New Testament world as in ours.

that there is quarreling among you, my brethren. This can only refer to the strife of competing loyalties and hostile ideologies. In

PAUL FOR TODAY'S CHURCH

Paul's concluding appeal to the Romans, he urges them to conduct themselves "becomingly as in the day, not in reveling and drunkenness, not in debauchery and licentiousness, not in quarreling and jealousy" (Rom 13:13). This, as readers of Saint Augustine's *Confessions* recognize, was the passage in which the young Augustine heard the voice urging him to "Pick up and read!" The rest of his life was an uninterrupted pageant of a life spent in responding to it in Hippo Regius.

1:12 What I mean is that each one of you says, "I belong to Paul," or "I belong to Apollos," or "I belong to Cephas," or "I belong to Christ." To obviate any mistaking his meaning in the preceding two verses, Paul gives examples of the phenomenon he laments. To do so, he, accomplished rhetorician that he was, has recourse to the rhetorical figure of climax or anabasis, listing the Corinthian slogans in ascending order of importance and, as he does elsewhere, putting himself at the lowest rank (1 Cor 15:8–9).

The evil of such factionalism, so much in vogue today in some theological circles, signifies not just the fragmentation of the fellowship, but also the inevitable slighting of the Lordship of Jesus Christ. For Paul, belonging to Christ is, and always has to be, indivisible and exclusive of all other allegiances.

1:13 Is Christ divided? Was Paul crucified for you? Or were you baptized in the name of Paul? The triad of rhetorical questions, of course, does not anticipate answers, the answer to each question being obvious. But each rhetorical question is an irrefutable challenge to the factional slogans proliferating in Corinth. That Christ is not "divided" rejects any and all division in the community. But that Christ, and no one else, died for them is the reason for their oneness and unity. Such unity is given expression in the baptismal rite. Having been baptized in the name of Christ, who died for them on the cross, the Corinthians had to be always on the lookout for any divisive gesture that would do injury to Christ, the sole source of their grace (1:4) and sanctification (1:2).

1:14–15 I am thankful that I baptized none of you except Crispus and Gaius; lest any one should say that you were baptized in my name. Such allegiance to the master who inducted them into one or another of the mystery cults with which most of the Gentile converts in Corinth were acquainted was, understandably enough, readily translated to the person who baptized them into the Christian religion. This is the reason for Paul's gratitude. His having baptized only two known members of the church at Corinth fended off the temptation to mistake the rite of their initiation as "in the name of Paul." Baptism is what it is only if it is in the name of Jesus Christ. Any other name would put it on a par with the pagan initiation rituals of the day.

1:16 (I did baptize also the household of Stephanas. Beyond that, I do not know whether I baptized any one else.) A lapse of memory, from which none of us, not even a sacred author, is exempt. The "household of Stephanas" was a well-known name in the Corinthian community. They were the first converts in Achaia, the region where Corinth is located (1 Cor 16:15). This makes Paul's lapse in memory almost unforgivable, though certainly quite comprehensible.

1:17 For Christ did not send me to baptize but to preach the gospel,... What priest in the Catholic Church, or what minister in any church, would muster the hardihood to utter such a forthright statement? Indeed, the reverse is likely, especially in Christian communities that have forgotten that the primary ministry is the ministry of the Word. Paul has no doubts on that score: "Woe to me if I do not preach the gospel" (1 Cor 9:16; Rom 15:26).

This compulsion to preach the gospel situates Paul and his ministry squarely within the prophetic ministry. He regarded his vocation to the ministry in a prophetic context (Gal 1:15; Isa 49:1; Jer 1:5). He also regarded his ministry of the Word, his preaching of the gospel, no less prophetically:

If I say, I will not mention him, or speak any more in
   his name,

there is in my heart as it were a burning fire shut up
   in my bones,
and I am weary with holding it, and I cannot.
   (Jer 20:9)

and not with eloquent wisdom, lest the cross of Christ be emptied of its power. This is a qualification all the more necessary in a Corinth as enamored of wisdom as of eloquence in all their forms and styles. It is perhaps hard for us today to imagine a populace in a thriving metropolitan center seeking their amusement and diversion in listening to orators in the marketplace or finding amusement in some philosophical discourse at a street corner. Paul himself was a rhetorician. This is an acquired art. But judging by his enemies' estimate of his abilities (2 Cor 10:10), he was no orator. Oratory is a cultivated but native talent.

Be that as it may, Paul takes his statement in an entirely different direction. Whether wise or not, whether eloquent or not, he is ever careful to preach the gospel in such a way as not to risk voiding the cross of Christ of its power. The cross was then, as it is now, an incomprehensible "folly." There have always been those in every generation who sought to get around this stumbling block or merely to bypass it altogether. Today, perhaps this latter attitude prevails. Amidst our cushy comforts and necessary luxuries, the cross is an unnecessary distraction. Nevertheless, it happens to be, in some circles at least, quite fashionable to use the cross in order to hold forth on violence and its sociology, anthropology, psychology, or what have you.

To Paul, the cross is a source of power: "it is the power of God for salvation to every one who has faith" (Rom 1:16). It is this which Paul proclaims that the power is God's, not his. Salvation is exclusively from God, and from no one else. Both the power and the salvation are paradoxically manifested in the weakness and the death on the cross. All attempts to bypass this or to attenuate its "folly" inevitably empties the cross of its power.

1:18 For the word of the cross is folly to those who are perishing, but to us who are being saved it is the power of God. There is an unsuspected twist in Paul's explanation of his meaning. First of all, those who regard the cross as folly, that is, who refuse to accept its power to save, do "perish." The verb in Greek is well rendered as "perish" to mean "utterly destroy," because to refuse the offer of life in salvation is to die. Period! So it is not as though a segment of the people has been doomed to destruction from the start, and consequently they deny the power of the cross. Such a view has been held off and on in times past and present. But this is what Paul does not, and cannot, say.

Should there be any doubt about his meaning, however, Paul goes on to reassure the believers that their faith in the cross as the power of God is indeed the sure sign of their "being saved." One must note the use of the passive verb here to stress what has already been stated, namely, salvation is exclusively God's work. As a totally free gift, it necessarily requires its recipient's totally free acceptance, that is, faith. This faith recognizes, at the very instant of its coming into existence, that it itself is no less a gift as well.

1:19 For it is written, "I will destroy the wisdom of the wise, and the cleverness of the clever I will thwart." Paul appeals here to Isaiah 29:14 (see Ps 33:10). Though the turn of phrase is unmistakably Semitic, the text as cited is from the Septuagint (LXX), the Greek version of the Old Testament. In order not to mistake the meaning of the Isaian text, we must keep in mind that, for God's holy people, nothing happens without the ultimate agency of God. They recognize a fact and attribute it to God as the first cause of all things: "I make weal, and create woe, I am the Lord, who do all these things" (Isa 45:7).

The wise and clever of this world might scoff at the glad tidings, reject the good news, refuse the gift of salvation, and incur the inevitable consequence. To the believer observing this, the phenomenon is another instance of "I will destroy the wisdom of the wise, and the cleverness of the clever I will thwart." This is an act of faith on the part of the believer, not a passing of judgment. Judgment belongs exclusively to God.

1:20 Where is the wise man? Where is the scribe? Where is the debater of this age? Has not God made foolish the wisdom of the world? It would be invidious to render the three categories of "wise man," "scribe," and "debater" into their easily identifiable counterparts in our age. They, like their predecessors, have one thing in common: to submit both the creator and creation to their superior criteria and thought processes. They discard whatever does not fit into their intellectual schemes or come up to their standards of judgment. Having once set their knowledge and competence as the measure by which all things, visible and invisible, human or divine, are to be assessed, they can only regard whoever takes a path other than their own as a misguided fool. This is what they determine to be in accord with their wisdom, all else being irretrievable foolishness.

What stiffens the resolve of such "wise men, scribes, and debaters of this age," and what hardens their disdainful intransigence is precisely the knowledge that the Almighty has "fixt his canon" against their haughtiness. They find the conviction of their opponents that God has in fact "made foolish the wisdom of the world" galling and intolerable, all the more so perhaps because time and again they have seen such conviction borne out.

1:21 For since, in the wisdom of God, the world did not know God through wisdom, it pleased God through the folly of what we preach to save those who believe. Paul gives the reason for his stated opinion unequivocally. The world did not, and does not, know God through wisdom. Paul's words here suggest that the attempt to construct a purely natural theology should take seriously his strictures on human wisdom. No one is disposed to ask what sort of God the wisdom of the world could come up with, let alone what relation this God bears to the God who, in the "folly" of the gospel, is preached to the believers of every age. This folly requires humble submission and ready obedience to the message proclaimed, and neither submission nor obedience sits well with the lofty pretension of the wisdom of the world. To forestall any misunderstanding on this point, Paul goes on to give concrete illustration of what he means:

1:22 *For Jews demand signs and Greeks seek wisdom,...* The demand for signs marked the progress of the holy people down the various stages of God's dealing with them. From "I am the Lord your God, who brought you out of the land of Egypt, out of the house of bondage" (Exod 20:2), the first great sign, down to "What sign have you to show us for doing this?" (John 2:18), this has been the mode of approach to the deity. It is, however, of the nature of the quest for signs to be insatiable. In its own way, the quest holds God, as it were, hostage to its extortionist demands, making the sign the condition for obedience and submission. Signs are all good and fine when they are positive, granted according to the heart's desires, when they bring the coveted gift or fulfill the ardent wish. But, be the sign vouchsafed negative, should it go counter to the expected result and the expected fulfillment, then the temptation to abandon God becomes almost insurmountable. It is all the more difficult to surmount the temptation to believe that it is in fact God who has abandoned his people, although in fact this is simply impossible: "Has God rejected his people? By no means!" (Rom 11:1).

By "Greeks," Paul understands all "non-Jews" in the inhabited world (compare 1 Cor 1:23). The path the Gentiles choose is that of the wondrous achievements of the human mind. The wisdom they seek had its dawning, not in the Hellenistic world of Paul, but farther east, a good millennium or two before. Wisdom has always been regarded with the greatest esteem, whether in Babylon, Memphis, Persepolis, or Athens. But, like all the products of human ingenuity, it bore the seeds of its undoing within itself. Wisdom in such a small creature as man can never be an end in itself. The temptation to self-sufficiency is bound to be its failure, however adept the wise are at explaining away this failure and limitation.

1:23 but we preach Christ crucified, a stumbling block to Jews and folly to Gentiles,... The crucified Christ is the negative sign par excellence for the Jews and utter folly for the Gentiles. By any human estimate, whether among God's own people or in the world at large, it is inexplicable folly. In a very real sense, the crucified Christ discloses the inherent limit of signs and lays bare the ultimate insufficiency of this world's wisdom. There comes a point when the signs must abandon their insatiable quest, and wisdom must relinquish its claim and utter its "O the depth of the riches and wisdom and knowledge of God! How unsearchable are his judgments and how inscrutable his ways!" (Rom 11:33).

1:24 but to those who are called, both Jews and Greeks,... It is seldom remarked that those who are called (see 1 Cor 1:1, 2, 9) are conclusive proof, were one needed, that neither the quest for signs nor the search for wisdom necessarily terminates there. There is always the moment when the futility of one and the inadequacy of the other will yield to the goal for which both the signs and wisdom were ultimately propaedeutics. At least one seeker after signs, and one not unacquainted with wisdom, came to a juncture when he could say, "But whatever gain I had, I counted as loss for the sake of Christ. Indeed I count everything as loss because of the surpassing worth of knowing Christ Jesus my Lord. For his sake I have suffered the loss of all things, and count them as refuse, in order that I may gain Christ" (Phil 3:7–8).

Christ the power of God and the wisdom of God. This, of course, is the crucified Christ who, in the stumbling block of the cross and in the folly of his death on it, reveals the true power and wisdom of God. Topsy-turvydom is the manner of God's dealings with humanity. Where they see only darkness, he shines his true light; what they judge as arrant foolishness, he discloses to be genuine wisdom. Our human hierarchies are stood on their head. Indeed, only in this upside-down position do human values acquire their true measure. The desire for signs is once and for all stilled, for God has given us "all things" with this Christ (Rom 8:32). The quest for wisdom finds its true fulfillment in him who destroys "the wisdom of the wise" (1 Cor 1:19), only to give us him "in whom are hid all the treasures of wisdom and knowledge" (Col 2:3).

1:25 For the foolishness of God is wiser than men, and the weakness of God is stronger than men. This is but the statement of the obvious. Of course, to those who are not called, God's way of acting in the cross is "weakness," a perceived failure to grant the sign they seek: "Come down from the cross" (Mark 15:30). What they sought was the sign of an ultimately victorious Messiah who triumphs once and for all over their enemies. The sign they get is the abject failure of the crucified: "But we had hoped that he was the one to redeem Israel" (Luke 24:21). But it is through that very failure and weakness, through the seeming stifling of hope, that the true power of God becomes permanently manifest.

So, too, among the Gentiles who are called, the whole catastrophe of the cross is sheer folly, a foreign superstition. Human wisdom would not have sought its objectives by such dead-end means. Human wisdom would have depleted all the resources of reasoning and diplomacy, of menace and hypocrisy ("You are not Caesar's friend....We have no king but Caesar"; John 19:12, 15). Human wisdom will know where to draw the line between assent and credulity. It likes nothing better than to spend its time in "telling or hearing something new" (Acts 17:21). When, in fact, the only really new thing comes its way, all that human wisdom can contrive to do is defer the moment indefinitely: "We will hear you again" sometime (Acts 17:32).

1:26 For consider your call, brethren; not many of you were wise according to worldly standards [according to the flesh], not many were powerful, not many were of noble birth;... A salutary reminder to all believers in all the churches and every age! To remember how and when we were called keeps our present status in perspective and serves as a constant reminder of the gratitude that must be ours for having been called. To be sure, Paul does not say that all who were called were not wise, or powerful, or of noble birth. Those who in fact were wise and powerful and of noble birth usually need no such reminders. Paul has in mind, principally, the majority, who came from humble backgrounds, those who ostensibly had little or nothing to recommend their choice. The point he makes is simply this: "The Lord sees not as man sees" (1 Sam 16:7).

We, and the Corinthians before us, would do well to reflect on the disciples the Lord chose during his public ministry. Who in the world, for instance, would have chosen a Peter, or a Thomas, or even a Paul (Gal 1:23)? The list of the Twelve reads like a roster of rejects in any worldly enterprise. God's choice always goes counter to the world's expectations and reckoning, whether in Corinth or in today's church, where this applies to popes and porters, to bishops and sacristans, to pastors and bell ringers. No calling is too lofty or too lowly to be included.

1:27 but God chose what is foolish in the world to shame the wise, God chose what is weak in the world to shame the strong. God, of course, still does. But, to our optic, his seems a losing battle. No sooner is anyone called for a particular task than he or she sets about to eradicate all traces of past foolishness and weakness from their lives, taking steps to ensure that the power that is theirs is bound to triumph, for it is, as they say, the "will of God." Proud of their newfound possession, some Corinthians were prompt to lord it over their fellow Christians, providing a sober counter-example for Christian leaders.

This is a theme to which Paul is bound to return in chapters 12—14 of First Corinthians, where he will treat, *ex professo*, the role of charisms in the church. When he does, this brief section, 1 Corinthians 1:26–31, must be constantly before the reader's eyes. The paradoxical principles of divine election enunciated in the concluding verses of 1 Corinthians 1 will undergird what Paul will say later about the call to service in the church.

1:28 God chose what is low and despised in the world, even things that are not, to bring to nothing things that are,... However reluc-

18

tant every one of us be to endorse such an austere view of divine election, we can never bypass it or, as happens more often, rationalize it away. The zeal and alacrity with which anyone called sets about to eradicate the traces of past lowliness and low esteem never ceases to be a cause for wonder. Part of their success is, inevitably, due to those whom they have been called to serve. It is not just love and admiration that motivates them, nor merely the desire to bask in some of the reflected glory, but the conviction that they deserve the very best to manage their church affairs. From the first century on, we have had ample opportunity to overthrow this verse, to nullify its force. So successful have we been that those called to serve—for God's call is always a call to serve—can conceive of their service only as service from above to those below. They serve always those beneath them. Never are they beneath those they serve: "For the Son of man also came not to be served but to serve" (Mark 10:45).

Of course, there are, and there have always been, exceptions. But these serve only to confirm the point, not refute it.

1:29 so that no human being [all flesh] might boast in the presence of God. The task upon which Paul and all his successors are engaged requires, before all else, the recognition of our creaturehood. When the Greek text says, as it does here, "all flesh," it means, as always in Paul, all that is not God, and therefore all that is created (compare 1 Cor 1:26). In the presence of its Creator, no creature, no "flesh," can ever boast. If it must boast at all, then the creature must "all the more gladly boast of [its] weakness" (2 Cor 12:9).

1:30 He is the source of your life in Christ Jesus,... God alone is the source of life. The life that is ours is, moreover, ours in Christ Jesus. The very life that is ours in Christ Jesus is a gift of God and, hence, not a cause for boasting but for gratitude (1 Cor 4:7). The realization of this fact, far from being a pious sentiment, must be the force that drives the Christian life forward: "It is no longer I who live, but Christ who lives in me; and the life I now live in the flesh I live by faith in the Son of God, who loved me and gave

19

himself for me" (Gal 2:20). This is precisely what Paul spells out in the rest of the verse:

[Christ Jesus] whom God made our wisdom, our righteousness and sanctification and redemption;... God is, as always and in everything, at the source. God, who is the Creator of creation, is also the author of our redemption in Christ Jesus, a redemption that is so compendiously described in its effects here. God made Christ our wisdom, for, as the psalmist sings, "In your light do we see light" (Ps 36:9; and see John 8:12). The wisdom that is ours in Christ Jesus is one that the world does not have to give, all its protestations to the contrary notwithstanding.

That Christ is "our righteousness and sanctification and redemption" is a multiple expression for the fact that he is our redeemer. He who by his death redeems us inevitably sets us in right relationship with God, and we become a precious possession of the Father ("You were bought with a price"; 1 Cor 6:20). This belonging to God is what our "sanctification" means. This is why we are "called to be saints" (1 Cor 1:2). Here again we find the basis on which all that follows in the epistle rests. We have come full circle, from "called to be saints" in 1:2 to "sanctification" in 1:30. This is another rhetorical device known as *inclusio*. In oral delivery, it marks the start and finish of a section audibly.

1:31 therefore, as it is written, "Let him who boasts, boast of the Lord." This is the inevitable conclusion to all that preceded. With this paraphrase of Jeremiah 9:22–23 (in the LXX), Paul reminds his readers that, if any one is disposed to boast—and who isn't?—then the boast must find its only true object in the Lord.

Chapter 2

FIRST CORINTHIANS 2

2:1 When I came to you, brethren, I did not come proclaiming to you the testimony [mystery] of God in lofty words or wisdom. The hold that wisdom had on the Corinthians was perhaps even more compelling than that of science in our time. Paul came to Corinth proclaiming the gospel of God. The English version reads the "testimony," while the Greek has "mystery"—in Greek manuscripts the discrepancy in reading is more readily comprehensible. In either reading, the gospel does both: it bears testimony (*martyria*) to God's act in Christ, and it proclaims the "gospel and the preaching of Jesus Christ, according to the revelation of the mystery (*mysterion*) which was kept secret for long ages" (Rom 16:25).

Mid the scramble for wisdom and the pursuit of learned orators in Corinth, Paul reminds the Corinthians of the way he himself proclaimed the gospel to them: neither in lofty words nor in wisdom. The essential of the proclamation is that it be comprehensible (1 Cor 14:19). Whatever the charm of words and the dazzle of wisdom, the essential is the communication of the good news so that it be genuinely good and truly intelligible news to the least in the congregation. Saint Augustine, great preacher though he was, reminded his hearers that he preferred offending the grammarians to leaving his people ignorant.

Paul's attitude is both laudable and intelligible. Yet there have never been wanting acerb critics who confounded clarity of expression with shallowness and simplicity of language with ignorance. Only a very brief while after Paul wrote these words to Corinth, his enemies in that city were using his lack of "lofty words or wisdom," even his physical appearance, to turn the com-

21

munity against him: "His letters are weighty and strong, but his bodily presence is weak, and his speech of no account" (2 Cor 10:10).

2:2 For I decided to know nothing among you except Jesus Christ and him crucified. This, if you pardon the pun, is the crux of the matter. It always comes back to the cross. It was then, and it is now, "a stumbling block to Jews and folly to Gentiles" (1 Cor 1:23). It ill becomes the bearers of the message of Jesus Christ crucified to level off the stumbling block and attenuate the folly of the cross with congenial contemporary theologies.

Once again, the reader of First Corinthians must keep in mind, if the epistle is to safeguard its true message, that the reason behind what Paul says, his answers to the Corinthian queries, and his reaction to the problems and crises in their community all find their source in Christ and him crucified. This, in every age, has served and will continue to serve as the badge of authenticity of the gospel message, and the only valid credential of its proclaimers.

2:3 And I was with you in weakness and in much fear and trembling;... These words describe well Paul's condition and the condition of so many who followed in his footsteps, who knew the paralyzing power of new situations, the intimidation of first-time encounters, and the tongue-tying effect of strangers. We, who endow the "apostle of the Gentiles" (Acts 13:47; 18:6) with suprahuman powers and imagine him equipped with every perfection, are not in a position to call into question his word in these few verses. Whatever quality Paul lacked, he did not lack that lucidity about himself that, being largely wanting in his critics as well as in his champions, makes them misjudge him and mistake his motives.

2:4 and my speech and my message were not in plausible words of wisdom,... These words only make more explicit what Paul has just said. The gospel he brought the Corinthians, as well as the idiom it was presented in, were unlike what the Corinthians were

22

accustomed to in their orators and itinerant philosophers. Paul must surely have heard of parables attributed to Jesus. He could well have had recourse to them in proclaiming the gospel. He certainly did not lack the genius with which interpreters through the ages expounded and disclosed the treasures of wisdom hidden within them. Yet Paul made not even a passing reference to them. Christ and him crucified was the gospel Paul preached without embellishment. How in fact he did this is admirably in evident in First Corinthians.

but in demonstration of the Spirit and of power,... Here we see where the real power of Paul's gospel resides. The reference to "the Spirit and...power" is yet another rhetorical device to express more forcefully what is usually described as "the power of the Spirit," which is itself a near-tautology, describing one thing by its synonym, because the Spirit is in fact power. What must be kept in mind, however, is that the demonstrable results of Paul's preaching in Corinth bear witness to the power of the Spirit, and not to Paul's prowess. If Paul's nonlofty words, his lack of "wisdom," his "weakness and much fear and trembling" did triumph in the end, then that triumph was the outcome of the power of the Spirit.

2:5 that your faith might not rest in the wisdom of men but in the power of God. This verse expresses the reason for all that has gone before. The Corinthians' faith does not, and could not, rest on the fluctuating fortunes of human wisdom any more than can any faith rest on the kaleidoscope of theological opinions in any age, but simply and solely on the "power of God," the Holy Spirit.

2:6 Yet among the mature we do impart wisdom, although it is not a wisdom of this age or of the rulers of this age, who are doomed to pass away. The understandable desire for wisdom often blinds its seekers to its true quality. The wisdom Paul brings to his hearers goes counter to all they have come to seek and expect in wisdom. Indeed, what Paul brings them seems more like genuine folly than

23

wisdom. It takes maturity of judgment to discern the true wisdom in the gospel message that Paul proclaims.

Today's situation can shed light on the matter. The wisdom the gospel preaches is decidedly not of this age, not of this world. Indeed, to the present age, it is sheer folly. It is a common enough sight to see Christian communities clamoring to have the gospel proclaimed in conformity with the wisdom of the present age. Any refusal to do so is regarded as benighted obscurantism. Each element in the gospel that goes counter to the prevailing wisdom of this world is dismissed as archaic.

Paul saw clearly the one distinguishing mark of the wisdom of the gospel vis-à-vis that of the world. The wisdom "of the age" is "doomed to pass away." Its very transience robs it of any genuine claim to wisdom. In today's rapid world of communication, one does not have to live a great number of years to see the chameleon alterations in intellectual fashions. "Yesterday's avant-garde experiment is today's chic and tomorrow's cliché," a far cry from "Jesus Christ is the same yesterday and today and for ever" (Heb 13:8).

2:7 But we impart a secret and hidden wisdom of God, which God decreed before the ages for our glorification. This wisdom is "secret and hidden" because it is not accessible to human intellectual efforts. Only God graciously concedes such wisdom, and that for our "glorification." For it is God "who has shone in our hearts to give the light of the knowledge of the glory of God in the face of Christ" (2 Cor 4:6). The response in faith to the gospel of Christ is our salvation (1 Cor 1:30) and our glorification: "Those whom he called he also justified; and those whom he justified he also glorified" (Rom 8:30). All that the world craves is on offer free of charge to anyone who has faith.

2:8 None of the rulers of this age understood this; for if they had, they would not have crucified the Lord of glory. How admirably forthright Paul is, and how very different from those who inherited his solicitude "for all the churches" (2 Cor 11:28). There are innumerable ways to "crucify the Lord of glory," and they did not cease with Calvary. The "rulers of this age," the mighty of the world and its trendsetters have never been slow to exploit them. Their ingenuity extends even to reshaping and redacting the Word of the cross to their own specifications. At times even church leaders fail to emphasize the importance of the cross in Christian life. Alas, "the sons of this world are more shrewd in dealing with their own generation than the sons of light" (Luke 16:8).

2:9 But, as it is written, "What no eye has seen, nor ear heard, nor the heart of man conceived, what God has prepared for those who love him,..." In this cento of citations from Isaiah (64:4; 52:15; 65:16), from Jeremiah (3:16), and even from the Old Testament Apocrypha (*Apocalypse of Elijah*), Paul has recourse to "what is written." In other words, he appeals to the Scriptures, both to clarify and to support his argument. The problem faced by all believers is precisely that of the visible versus the invisible, of the present versus that which is to come. The life of the Christian between the times, between this age and the age to come, inevitably poses problems, perhaps none of which is greater than that of the present tangible reality of the world. If the gospel message encounters almost insurmountable obstacles in its path, it is because, at every turn, it has to reckon with the very demonstrable reality of this world and its almost irresistible attraction. "The world," wrote Saint Augustine, "is full of trouble, yet loved; what if it were pleasing? How would you delight in its calms, that can so well endure its storms?" This is the very world at the heart of which the gospel must be proclaimed.

Paul's pastoral astuteness and human finesse come to the fore in this verse. In his *Rule*, Saint Benedict reminded the abbot to be temperate in the exercise of his authority, lest the weak draw back in alarm and the strong have nothing to strive after, even as Saint Paul reminds the Corinthians of what "God has prepared for those who love him." By comparison with the evanescent (1 Cor

2:6) proffered utopias of ages past and present, the divine promise is the only secure hope.

2:10 God has revealed to us through the Spirit. This is no more than the explicitation of what Paul had said in 2:6–7. The wisdom he proclaims is a revealed wisdom, a "secret and hidden wisdom," not of this world. The agent of this revelation is the Spirit. Nor is this action a once-for-all operation, but an ongoing process that we know by the name of "tradition" (1 Cor 11:23; 15:3).

For the Spirit searches everything, even the depths of God. This is a hyperbolic mode of expressing the limitless extent of the permeating power of the Spirit. This description of the properties of the revealing Spirit need not surprise us at this juncture. It is this power of the Spirit that puts in its true perspective the wisdom of this age (1 Cor 2:6). It is what enables the believers to judge the flummery of the world at its true worth. The Spirit's is always a disturbing presence in the world. The proclamation of the gospel message must always keep in mind, as well as in the mind of its hearers, the true source of the wisdom it brings. This is all the more necessary because its message will always be "a stumbling block to Jews and folly to Gentiles" (1 Cor 1:23).

2:11 For what person knows a man's thoughts except the spirit of the man which is in him? So also no one comprehends the thoughts of God except the Spirit of God. Paul has recourse to a comparison in order to explain what he has just said, that "the Spirit reaches...even the depth of God." The comparison, albeit an imperfect one, as all comparisons between the divine and the human are bound to be, simply compares the way one knows himself and the way the Spirit of God comprehends the thoughts of God. The RSV's "what person" is a periphrasis of the Greek "who," the intrusion of "person" into this particular context is ill advised. Yet future generations will not fail to discover in the verse hitherto unsuspected trinitarian riches, where "person" will come to play a major role.

26

2:12 Now we have received not the spirit of the world, but the Spirit which is from God, that we might understand the gifts bestowed on us by God. The verse goes on to explain the reason why Paul needed to remind his readers that "no one comprehends the thoughts of God except the Spirit of God." To do so, he rings the changes on a number of meanings that the "spirit" (*pneuma*) can have. There is the neutral sense of the term, as in "spirit of man," part of the biblical response to the psalmist's "What is man?" (Ps 8:4), which is technically called biblical anthropology. There is also the negative sense of "spirit," as in "the spirit of the world." This designation stands in marked contrast to all that the Spirit of God encompasses. The Spirit of God is the agent of revelation (1 Cor 2:10) and is in stark contrast with the spirit of the world (2:12). The Spirit of God makes us comprehend and acknowledge the gifts bestowed on us by God (2:12), that is, all that the event of Christ Jesus brings us ("He who did not spare his own Son but gave him up for us all, will he not also give us all things with him?" Rom 8:32). Just how very important this role of the Spirit is will become even clearer when Paul comes to treat the gifts of God in 1 Corinthians 12—14.

2:13 And we impart this in words not taught by human wisdom but taught by the Spirit,... Paul here cites but one of the gifts of the Spirit: the proclamation of the gospel. The verse comes back to the obsession of the Corinthians with "human wisdom" and the stumbling block that is the folly at the heart of the Christian message. It makes explicit what Paul had said about the revelatory function of the Spirit: "God has revealed to us through the Spirit" (1 Cor 2:10). How reluctant Christians are, whose vision stops short at the shortcomings of the bearer of the message, to reflect on this given of the faith in the context especially of Christian preaching from the lowliest of pulpits to the most exalted of cathedra!

interpreting spiritual truths to those who possess the Spirit. The alliterativeness of this half-verse is even more striking in the

Greek text. It describes to perfection the task Paul undertakes in his epistles, and in First Corinthians in particular. This description of Paul's task is, at the same time, a prescription for all who undertake to proclaim and elucidate the meaning of the gospel to the believers. It applies equally to catechists as to teachers, to preachers, biblical interpreters, theologians, and doctors of the church. Time was when all those who undertook such a task unfailingly prefaced it with a prayer to the Holy Spirit, that all, teachers and taught, may "rightly savor" the "gifts bestowed on us by God" (1 Cor 2:12).

2:14 The unspiritual [natural] man does not receive the gifts of the Spirit of God, for they are folly to him, and he is not able to understand them because they are spiritually discerned. The RSV starts a new paragraph with this verse, but needlessly. Paul is continuing the same argument and is providing here an added reason for his position. The Greek term rendered here as "unspiritual" or "natural" is *psychikos*, which transliterated into English "psychic" carries with it wholly misleading connotations. It is sufficient for understanding Paul's argument here to see "unspiritual" in utter contrast to "spiritual" (*pneumatikos*, "pneumatic").

Once again, within the context of wisdom and folly, we are reminded that only those who possess the Spirit, that is, only the believers, can understand the gospel message and surmount the "folly" it proclaims. The good news requires the gift of the Spirit both in order to be accepted and to be comprehended. The act of faith must be both intelligent and intelligible, however paradoxical its content. The folly of the cross yields its true wisdom only to those who possess the Spirit.

2:15 The spiritual man judges all things, but is himself to be judged by no one. The spiritual man certainly may not be judged by anyone who is worldly, unspiritual. The believer who spiritually discerns the gifts of God has eyes to discern all things else at their true worth. The eyes of faith discover in this world "whatever is true, whatever is honorable, whatever is just, whatever is pure, whatever is lovely" (Phil 4:8). The spiritual individual does this with serene and unshakable confidence, even if the unspiritual, the worldly powers that be, determine, in their vaunted wisdom, to be the acceptable fashion of the day. The spiritual has the courage to call by its name all the world's lies, pettiness, injustices, squalor, and downright ugliness.

2:16 "For who has known the mind of the Lord so as to instruct him?" But we have the mind of Christ. Once again, as in 1:19 and 2:9, Paul appeals to Scripture to clinch this argument. Here, too, he cites Isaiah 40:13, Jeremiah 23:18, and Wisdom 9:13. The same sentiment finds expression both in the prophets and in wisdom literature. The sacred authors simply acknowledge the sovereign wisdom of the Lord. That we ourselves have "the mind of Christ" provides the reason for our recognition of the Lord's wisdom and, at the same time, fortifies us against the menacing forces of the world and all its efforts to disclose our folly. To have the mind of Christ is to have the mind of him who is "the power of God and the wisdom of God" (1 Cor 1:14).

Chapter 3

FIRST CORINTHIANS 3

3:1 But I, brethren, could not address you as spiritual men, but as men of the flesh, as babes in Christ. Christian proclamation is a pedagogy. In the welter of opinions on wisdom, Paul needed to remind the Corinthians that he had no choice but to address them as beginners, which is precisely what they were. They were like children progressing gradually to maturity. To advance from their "nonspiritual" (what Paul here calls "fleshly" *sarkinos*) status to the "spiritual," the status of maturity in Christ, is necessarily a gradual process. "Yet among the mature we do impart wisdom" (1 Cor 2:6). The Corinthians and their heirs down the ages disdained being addressed as "babes in Christ." They regarded themselves as a class apart, a race exempt from the limitations of both human and divine pedagogy. They expected to be addressed as "cognoscenti," on equal footing with the "professionals." There has never been wanting those who flatter the ignorance of such audiences, offering them knowledge well beyond their capacity to understand, and conferring upon them accolades of competence they could scarcely possess. Such an attitude is a reflex reaction to what we find in the following verse.

3:2 I fed you with milk, not solid food; for you were not ready for it; and even yet you are not ready,... However self-evident the truth of these words, one cannot overlook the fact that the proclaimers of the Word, more often than not, offered the believers a steady diet of "milk," thus fixating the faithful in an infantile stage that forever turns to those above them for answers to their questions, even questions to which the faithful themselves possess more expert and more authoritative competence.

The example set here by Paul, difficult as it is to emulate, seems to have counted for naught in the majority of cases that came after him. He realized that his proclamation was suited to the capacity of his audience, neither belittling their intelligence nor flattering their ignorance. Most of his audience came from Gentile backgrounds and had little, if anything, to prepare them for the gospel. They were, by and large, not naturally Christian souls. Since they were not yet ready for "solid food," he fed them with "milk." But, once they had emerged from their pupilarity, he did not hesitate to offer them the solid food that has nurtured mature Christians over the centuries. The First Letter to the Corinthians is a superb example of such mature fare for the Christians of every generation.

3:3 *for you are still of the flesh.* This verse makes explicit the reason Paul needed to add "and even yet you are not ready." As long as the Corinthians think and behave in unspiritual, that is, "fleshly" or "worldly" ways, they betray their unreadiness for more solid instruction. The world at this juncture rushes in to accentuate their prejudices, confirm them in their ill-formed judgments, multiply their divisions, and increase their opposition to anyone who sees them for what they are: "babes" tossed hither and yon by the mutable fashions of the age. Paul goes on to make explicit the meaning of this phrase.

For while there is jealousy and strife among you, are you not of the flesh, and behaving like ordinary men? Jealousy and strife mark the realm of the flesh. Paul regards "flesh" (*sarx*) not merely in its common acceptation in everyday usage but rather as a realm of all that is created and mutable, of all that is not God, and all that can be opposed to God. "Spirit" (*pneuma*), in addition to its ordinary denotations, is the realm of the Creator. It is what Paul calls the pneumatic (spiritual) realm, as distinguished from the sarkic (fleshly).

It is astonishing how unwilling Christians are to see the jealousy and strife that pervade the world as undeniable signs of its opposition to the Creator. It is even more astonishing how ready they are to accept the world's premise that precisely such jealousy

31

and strife is the mark of maturity. A long time ago, H. de Lubac remarked that it is not that the world cannot organize itself without God, but that, without God, it can only organize itself against man. Of course, the tools for this organization are jealousy and strife.

3:4 *For when one says, "I belong to Paul," and another, "I belong to Apollos," are you not merely men?* Of course, they are! The RSV adds "merely" here and in 3:3, and rightly so, although the Greek has only "men," without any qualifier. Paul reminds the Corinthians that their behavior shows them singularly lacking in precisely what they prize so highly in the new religion, spiritual gifts (see 1 Cor 12). He insists that, as long as factions and divisions are in evidence in their community, they are really babes and not mature (2:6). They are "unspiritual [natural] men" (2:14), and certainly not *pneumatic* (2:15) men able to understand the gifts of the Spirit of God (2:14).

After more than two thousand years, Christians are still slow to see the truth in this verse. Is it possible for anyone today to think of a fellow Christian without pigeonholing her or him as either liberal or conservative, as belonging to this faction or that, as espousing this outlook or another? How many today are willing to judge the phenomenon as Paul judged its twin in Corinth? It is quite incomprehensible how ready Christians are to glory in the world's applause of their divisions and factions, their jealousy and strife, and their outright refusal to be anything but merely men, heedless of the supernal call of God in Christ Jesus (see Phil 3:14).

3:5 *What then is Apollos? What is Paul? Servants through whom you believed, as the Lord assigned to each.* This is a much-needed reminder, not only to the Corinthians, but also to every generation of believers. Those who minister the Word to the community are nothing but its servants. If the ministers themselves need such a reminder, the believers need it much more. One of the preeminent titles of the pope is "Servant of the Servants of God." If, perchance, the holder of the supreme office should believe this, few, if any, of his subjects are even willing to contemplate it.

32

The essential here is the reminder that it is the Lord who assigns the ministers and allots the ministries. He alone is the source of the entire task of the proclamation from its inception to its consummation.

3:6 *I planted, Apollos watered, but God gave the growth.* The verse only confirms that the primacy in the ministry is to be accorded to God alone. If one were to adapt Saint Augustine's famous dictum on grace, "Without us, God will not; without God, we cannot," one can assess the work of the ministry at its true worth. God wills to have ministers to carry out the task of the ministry, whether the minister be Paul or Apollos or whoever. But no minister can ever forget that the task, from start to finish, from spring sowing to autumnal harvest, is God's work. Necessary, even indispensable, though Paul and Apollos and their like be, the ultimate source of their endeavors and their achievements is God:

3:7 *So neither he who plants nor he who waters is anything, but only God who gives the growth.* This is all the more difficult to accept in our Pelagian times, with the elevation of numero uno to hitherto unconceived eminence, and the unprecedented triumph of the me generation over all the rhetoric of altruism.

3:8 *He who plants and he who waters are equal, and each shall receive his wages according to his labor.* Paul hastens to forestall an objection. What he said in 3:5–7 was not meant to discount the very real work of the laborers. It remains true in all circumstances that without human agency, without the prophets, the apostles, the preachers, the teachers, "without us, God will not." This is not merely divine condescension, but the working out of the logic of creation: "Let us make man in our image, after our likeness" (Gen 1:26).

3:9 *For we are God's fellow workers; you are God's field, God's building.* This goes well beyond "in our image, after our likeness." The ministers are, literally, collaborators with God. All the sometimes cruel appearances to the contrary notwithstanding, the minister is never alone, never solitary. Circumstances may sometimes conspire to obscure this fact, but it remains inalterably true.

Paul, in keeping with the agricultural tropes he uses in 5:6, 7, and 8—"planted...watered"—reminds the Christians that they are "God's field" under tillage, where the ministers of the Word plant and water and tend the land (see the Parable of the Sower in Mark 4:3–9 and its parallels in Matthew and Luke). But he adds another, more important, trope: "God's building [*oikodomē*]." Whereas *field* is used but once in Paul and, indeed, nowhere else in the New Testament, *building* is very frequent (1 Cor 14:3, 5, 12; 2 Cor 5:1; 10:8; 12:19; 13:10). It is difficult not to see Paul intentionally adding this image here. For, later on, in 1 Corinthians 14, he will take it up in dealing with the topic of teaching and preaching the Word as divine gifts at the service of the community. In 1 Corinthians 14, as here in chapter 3, problems have arisen precisely on this subject. But, whereas in 1 Corinthians 3 the problems arose on the part of the Corinthians themselves, in 1 Corinthians 14 they are on the part of those who proclaimed the Word to them.

3:10 According to the grace of God given to me, like a skilled master builder I laid a foundation, and another man is building upon it. Let each man take care how he builds upon it. The image of the builder is carried further. Paul, as the founder of the Corinthian church, laid its foundations. He will, consequently, always feel responsible for its welfare, even as his successors will promote its growth. He knows himself to be a "skilled" (the Greek in fact uses "wise," perhaps harking back to the topic of wisdom) "architect." The term is literally what the Greek vocable says. Such open-eyed recognition of his skill and achievement, far from contradicting what he has just said in 3:5–8, admirably illustrates its true meaning. As a once-famous ecclesiastic insisted during a debate in Vatican I, God will not take away from man what man can do. Nevertheless, God is ever the architect who builds with "transitory tools" (*per machinas transituras*) an abiding edifice, as Saint Augustine puts it.

The other man building on the foundation Paul laid down is, in all likelihood, Apollos. If he is the same Apollos as the one described in Acts, then we can glean the following facts about him:

> Now a Jew named Apollos, a native of Alexandria, came to Ephesus. He was an eloquent man, well versed in the scriptures. He had been instructed in the way of the Lord; and being fervent in spirit, he spoke and taught accurately the things concerning Jesus, though he knew only the baptism of John. He began to speak boldly in the synagogue; but when Priscilla and Aquila heard him, they took him and expounded to him the way of God more accurately. And when he wished to cross to Achaia, the brethren encouraged him, and wrote to the disciples to receive him. When he arrived, he greatly helped those who through grace had believed, for he powerfully confuted the Jews in public, showing by the scriptures that the Christ was Jesus. (Acts 18:24–28)

Nothing Paul says about Apollos in First Corinthians contradicts the biographical data in Acts. If this be so, then, according to 1 Corinthians 16:12, Apollos, too, will have left Corinth (Acts 19:1) by the time this epistle was written. This is perhaps the reason why Paul feels the need to add, "Let each man take care how he builds upon it."

3:11 For no other foundation can any one lay than that which is laid, which is Jesus Christ. The warning appended to the previous verse is not to ward off intruders but to define a territory christologically. Paul is not defending his claims as an apostle, but safeguarding the integrity of the gospel. The edifice this master builder and his successors raised can have no other foundation except Jesus Christ. Human ingenuity has not been slow to provide other foundations more in accord with the prevalent fashions

of the day. The history of the expired twentieth century can furnish abundant examples of "master builders" raising monumental
"Christian" edifices on foundations other than Jesus Christ, and
the twenty-first bids fair to surpass it.

*3:12–13 Now if any one builds on the foundation with gold, silver,
precious stones, wood, hay, straw—each man's work will become
manifest;...* Time will never fail to reveal the true nature of the
edifice raised. Even the most seemingly indestructible can col-
lapse overnight. Even those that promised a thousand-year reign
tumbled into rubble. And even those that now seem everlasting to
us, as previous habitations seemed to their denizens, will pass. To
Paul and his followers, that building alone, which has Jesus Christ
for its foundation, will stand: "When some traveller from New
Zealand shall, in the midst of a vast solitude, take his stand on a
broken arch of London Bridge, to sketch the ruins of St. Paul's."

*for the Day will disclose it, because it will be revealed with fire, and
the fire will test what sort of work each one has done.* We are too
ready to forget Paul's habit of thinking eschatologically. Not only
the language he uses here, but his own conviction of the proximity of the end, dictate his choice of words. Regardless of the inac-
curacy of his expectations, the truth of what he says remains
unchallenged. Edifices raised on any foundation other than Jesus
Christ are bound to be revealed for what they are. However
unfashionable such a view of things may seem today, it remains
the unshakable conviction of one whose life and passion is "Jesus
Christ and him crucified" (1 Cor 2:1; 1:23).

A word of caution might well be useful at this juncture. Just
as we should be attentive to Paul's habits of thought, so must we
be aware of the parameters of his thinking. Paul is not writing
about comparative religions, nor is he undertaking an apology of
the Christian religion. He is an apostle of Christ, solicitous of the
integrity of the faith of his fellow Christians. No one in his right
mind would choose to deny him, or any other apostle, prophet, or

teacher, this privilege, which is rightly his. Yet, the number of those who do has been legion.

3:14–15 If the work which any man has built on the foundation survives, he will receive a reward. If any man's work is burned up, he will suffer loss, though he himself will be saved, but only as through fire. I have to confess at the outset that the meaning of these two verses escapes me. Nor are they the only verses in this epistle to do so. There seems to be a sudden shift in Paul's line of reasoning. Clearly, anyone who has built on the true foundation will see his edifice survive, as does Paul's in Corinth. The "reward" to be received is hard to opine, unless what Paul has in mind here is what he wrote to the Thessalonians: "For what is our hope or joy or crown of boasting before our Lord Jesus at his coming? Is it not you? For you are our glory and joy" (1 Thess 2:19–20). Could the reward he receives be precisely "the church of God which is at Corinth" (1 Cor 1:2), which is certainly his "joy and crown" (Phil 4:1)?

That anyone will "suffer loss" if his "work is burned up" is a truism. But the rest of the verse is puzzling. Like many such verses in the Scriptures, it has provided the basis for outlandish doctrines of every sort. But, confronted by the evident obscurity of the verse, one can only invoke the celebrated injunction of Wittgenstein: "Whereof one cannot speak, thereof one must be silent."

3:16 Do you not know that you are God's temple and that God's Spirit dwells in you? The reader emerges from the penumbra of the preceding two verses into the splendor of light. All that Paul had said about foundation and building now finds its culmination in this major affirmation of the epistle: "You are God's temple." The church of Corinth, built on the foundation of Jesus Christ, is in fact God's temple. This is the reason why, right from the start, Paul addresses the Corinthians as "those sanctified in Christ Jesus, called to be saints" (1:2). As has already been noted, their title to sanctity is not a consequence of their piety but of their belonging to God. They are *God's* temple.

Paul carries the statement a step further, making explicit what is already implied in it. He reminds the Corinthians of the obvious: in God's temple, the Spirit of God dwells. This is another of those derelict notions on the heap of pious irrelevancies. For, in their voluble discourse on the Spirit, Christians all too often overlook the fact that the Spirit dwelling within each of the believers must, inevitably, dictate the way each one thinks and lives. The believers, thus, have to "walk by the Spirit" (Gal 5:16, 25; Rom 8:4). All that Paul has to say in the following chapters about the conduct of Christians will have for its premise the fact that each believer is the temple of the Spirit, wherein the Spirit of God dwells.

3:17 If any one destroys God's temple, God will destroy him. For God's temple is holy, and that temple you are. The minatory accents of the first part of the verse are, evidently, prophetic. Paul, like Jesus and his followers, learned his idiom from the Scriptures of his youthful piety. The truth in this verse and in similar utterances is not, and can never be, license to take the threatened destruction into one's own hands. Those who destroy God's temple have God to deal with and no one else.

The second part of the verse makes explicit what the first part said: God's temple is holy because it belongs to God. To say something is holy, or sacred, is to say that it belongs to God. The fact that the temple is "you," is each individual member of the Corinthian community, hardly needs saying, yet Paul says it nevertheless, so important is it for understanding much of what will follow.

That every individual is a temple of God might seem self-evident, and yet, among all of today's rhetoric on human rights and human dignity, its truth is simply overlooked. That God, and even the more innocuous vocable "temple," are not in vogue could explain the neglect but cannot justify it. Might not such neglect be at the basis of all the mounting disregard for human dignity and human rights in our world?

38

3:18 Let no one deceive himself. If any one among you thinks that he is wise in this age, let him become a fool that he may become wise. Back to the theme of wisdom and folly we turn for one final reminder. The exhortation does not necessarily mean that no one in Corinth was in fact wise. They need not all have been mistaken. Some among them were indeed "wise in this age." What Paul wants them all to bear in mind is that, in order to receive the wisdom of the gospel, they need first to "become fools." This is particularly difficult for those who are wise in this age. You can almost hear them say, *This is an enlightened age. Surely, you cannot expect us to believe such superstition anymore.* Nevertheless, in every century, you must become a fool in order to become wise. This is the indispensable folly of the gospel, as Paul goes on to explain.

3:19–20 For the wisdom of this world is folly with God. Surprising though the statement sounds, it is almost a commonplace. Our language has many variants on the theme: "God's ways are not our ways"; "Man proposes, God disposes"; and so on. The continuous temptation is to say, reductively, *If I were God, I wouldn't have done it this way.* Such temptation is particularly persistent among professional theologians, who are prone to prescribe how God acts. In our time, the temptation is more likely to take the form of: *No good and just God could have done this!* or, better still, *If there is a God, this wouldn't have happened.* Thus, with the wisdom of the age, the wise in this age do away with what they judge to be folly, as well as with its author, becoming thus fools indeed.

For it is written, "He catches the wise in their craftiness," and again, "The Lord knows that the thoughts of the wise are futile." Once again, Paul calls upon the Scriptures to sum up and round off his line of argument. In the first citation, his appeal is to Job: "He frustrates the devices of the crafty, so that their hands achieve no success. He takes the wise in their own craftiness; and the schemes of the wily are brought to a quick end" (Job 5:12–13). In the second, he has recourse to the inexhaustible treasure of the Psalms: "The LORD knows the thoughts of man, that they are but a breath" (94:11). In both quotations, Paul once again cites the Septuagint (LXX), the Greek version of the Old Testament.

3:21-23 So let no one boast of men. The conclusion from the scriptural citation is obvious. It goes counter to the prevalent attitude of the Corinthians and their cult of personalities: "I belong to Paul," or "I belong to Apollos," or "I belong to Cephas" (1 Cor 1:12). Such factions and divisions in the community have been a continuous phenomenon in history. The list of heresies, no less than that of orthodoxies, reads like a doxographic who's who.

Apart the fissiparous consequences of such "boasting," it inevitably constricts the limitless horizons of each Christian's freedom. Few indeed are those who boast of one hero and yet remain open to others, or fail to take up arms against all others. This is the reason why Paul immediately goes on to add:

For all things are yours, whether Paul or Apollos or Cephas or the world or life or death or the present or the future,... The sudden shift from individuals to abstractions in the list, "world...life... death," is meant to show the universality of all the things possessed. This is a breathtaking restoration of the image of that first Adam as he issued forth from the hand of God. To possess all these is to enjoy genuine freedom. But to be possessed by any one of them is inescapable slavery. This is why this passage has been rightly called "the mightiest expression of Christian freedom"!

all are yours; and you are Christ's; and Christ is God's. The reiteration of "All things are yours" ought to call attention to our reluctance to believe this simple truth. The reason for our possessing all things is simply the fact of our belonging to Christ. We are Christ's possession and, consequently, know that all things are ours. The reason we possess all these things is that Christ himself belongs to God, who gave them and him to us: "He who did not spare his own Son but gave him up for us all, will he not also give us all things with him?" (Rom 8:32). In this same passage of Romans, Paul goes on to add a faithful echo of our Corinthian passage:

First Corinthians 3

For I am sure that neither death, nor life, nor angels, nor principalities, nor things present, nor things to come, nor powers, nor height, nor depth, nor anything else in all creation, will be able to separate us from the love of God in Christ Jesus our Lord. (Rom 8:38–39)

Chapter 4

FIRST CORINTHIANS 4

4:1 This is how one should regard us, as servants of Christ and stewards of the mysteries of God. The antidote to the factionalism in Corinth is a right estimate of those who "labor among you and are over you in the Lord and admonish you" (1 Thess 5:12). Whether the person in question be Cephas or Apollos or Paul or anyone else, they are all, without exception, to be regarded as servants of Christ, ministering to his people the mysteries it is their duty to proclaim. To regard such individuals as ministers and stewards is not to disdain and look down upon them but to appreciate their work and position in the community at its true worth: "to esteem them very highly in love because of their work" (1 Thess 5:13).

Would that it were unnecessary to add that, however, the servants and stewards in the community ought themselves never to forget what they are about, and not to lord it over those whom they are called (1 Cor 1:1) to serve. One can only wonder at the spectacle in history of how ordinary mortals have managed to bypass this reminder and set out to demonstrate all the evils of ostentatious power in its exercise of unbridled tyranny over the people.

4:2 Moreover it is required of stewards that they be found trustworthy. The criterion by which the servant of any community is to be judged is trustworthiness or, to reflect more closely the Greek term used, *faithfulness, fidelity.* The fidelity is, by the nature of things, in two directions: fidelity toward the God who called, equipped, and sent the ministers to serve his people; and fidelity toward the people themselves, jealously guarding the integrity of

the gospel they proclaim to them and vigilantly guiding their footsteps in its path.

Although delusion in the first aspect, fidelity toward God, is
easy to come by and not very difficult to sustain, the perversion of
the second aspect is almost endemic. It is so very easy for the servants and stewards of the community to confound their preferences and prejudices with the will of God. Nothing can be easier
than to declare one's personal views as genuine elements of the
revelation, especially if such views reflect the fashions of the day
and win the applause of the world:

> Thus says the Lord of hosts: "Do not listen to the words
> of the prophets who prophesy to you, filling you with
> vain hopes; they speak visions of their own minds, not
> from the mouth of the Lord. They say continually to
> those who despise the word of the Lord, 'It shall be well
> with you'; and to every one who stubbornly follows his
> own heart, they say, 'No evil shall come upon you.'"
> (Jer 23:16–17)

Yet it is easier still to betray one's stewardship toward the
community. It is easy enough to pretend that everything one does
is for the community, particularly if it be done with a view to
pleasing them, flattering their egos, playing up to their prejudices.
The very adaptability of the gospel message facilitates the wayward task of betraying its stewardship.

*4:3 But with me it is a very small thing that I should be judged by
you or by any human court.* This is the perennial temptation of all
those who minister to the community. It is the reason why Paul
always insists that he is "called by the will of God" (1 Cor 1:1),
that he is an apostle, that is, someone sent "not from men nor
through man, but through Jesus Christ and God the Father" (Gal
1:1). The call, "not from men nor through man," is the guarantee
of Paul's liberty in proclaiming the gospel. If this call is from God
and through Jesus Christ, then the one called is accountable to no

one else. Paul does not dismiss being judged by the Corinthians out of disdain for them, but simply from his awareness of the fact that they are impotent to pass such judgment, all their pretensions to the contrary notwithstanding. The community of believers lacks the power to judge because they lack the power to call. Confusion on this point of the ministry is at the root of countless evils in the church, whether in Achaia or in America.

I do not even judge myself. No human court can exceed in severity the inner court we set up within us. Not only is this inner court unsparing in condemnation and parsimonious in pity, it is forever in session. Once again, the only effective antidote to its tyranny is to remember that the origin of our call is solely and uniquely in God, through Jesus Christ. To forget this unique source of our freedom in the ministry is to fall into the thralldom of judgment by others, or into the ever more crippling slavery of judgment on ourselves. The effective antidote to this is Paul's salutary reminder of that much-forgotten "beatitude": Blessed is the one "who has no reason to judge himself for what he approves" (Rom 14:22).

4:4 I am not aware of anything against myself, but I am not thereby acquitted. It is the Lord who judges me. Judgment and acquittal in the ministry and its stewardship is exclusively in the hand of God. Unfortunately, church members and leaders have sometimes attempted to exercise the judgment that belongs to God.

4:5 Therefore do not pronounce judgment before the time, before the Lord comes, who will bring to light the things now hidden in darkness and will disclose the purposes of the heart. The horizon of the Christian's vision is always, or must always be, eschatological, always defined by the day when "the Lord comes." The light of that day will disclose all the things that are hidden deep in each heart. Only these deeply hidden verities can make up the true stuff of just judgment. The impenetrable darkness of the human heart guards its secret well from the eyes of tribunals and inquisitions. All the astute jurisprudence of this world cannot "disclose the purpose of the heart," "for the Lord sees not as man sees; man looks on the outward appearance, but the Lord looks on the heart" (1 Sam 16:7).

Then every man will receive his commendation from God. God is the sole infallible judge, and therefore unfailingly just. Not only does he pass judgment of condemnation, but he also makes the commendation that discloses the true worth of what, all too often, is despised and deemed worthless by the judges of this earth. Paul's insistence on the commendatory aspect of the divine judgment is always a salutary corrective to all those embroiled in the trammels of ecclesiastical politics. To do one's work in the church with one eye on pleasing the powers that be, ever on the alert for marks of disapproval, is a sterile servitude to those who do not, nor cannot, see as God sees. Very few of us reflect on the deleterious effects of such slavery in the proclamation of the gospel. Not only does it inevitably falsify its true focus, but it sacrifices its lucidity to the circumlocutions of churchly jargon and moribund clichés.

There is but one remedy to this endemic malaise, whether in the church of the Corinthians or in ours, and that is to seek one's "commendation" from God and from no one else. This is by no means easy to do all the time, but one has to think of the alternative. Those who labor in the church must ever find their freedom in "Who shall bring any charge against God's elect? It is God who justifies; who is to condemn?" (Rom 8:33–34).

4:6 *I have applied all this to myself and Apollos for your benefit, brethren, that you may learn by us not to go beyond what is written,...* The lucidity with which Paul makes his plea to the Corinthians is a model for the exercise of the ministry of the Word, an exercise that has failed to find much success in the church of any age. Paul applies his instruction, first and foremost, to himself and his fellow workers in the ministry in order that they may learn how to revel in "what is written" and not go beyond it in idle speculation and sterile hypotheses. The service Paul and his fellow missionaries render the community of believers is exemplified always in their own lives no less than expressed in their words. How the proclaimers apply the gospel message to themselves is every bit as essential as their catechesis and exhortation. "You know what kind of men we proved to be among you for your sake. And you became imitators of us and of the Lord" (1 Thess 1:5–6).

that none of you may be puffed up in favor of one against another. A sure safeguard against the factionalism of "I belong to Paul," or "I belong to Apollos," or "I belong to Cephas" (1 Cor 1:12) is the fact that each of them must be careful to apply the gospel to himself and to make sure "not to go beyond what is written." It is this trespassing beyond the bounds of what is written into personal ideologies and espoused philosophical systems that is at bottom the cause of all the multiple allegiances and factions in Corinth or any church elsewhere.

4:7 *For who sees anything different in you? What have you that you did not receive? If then you received it, why do you boast as if it were not a gift?* These words go to the heart of the problem. The believers in every age, whether in Paul's or in ours, and in every place, whether in Corinth or Rome or London or Rio de Janeiro, must always recognize that all that they have, everything they possess, is a gift of God. The recognition of this incontestable fact guards them not only against empty boasting but also from false associations. The fragmentation of communities, the division of loyalties, the conflict of warring factions in any church are but the manifestation of this tendency to forget the divine munificence at the bottom of all they are and all they possess. Boasting of their accomplishments and their allegiances is always a refusal to acknowledge the gifts they have received. "Let him who boasts, boast of the Lord" (1 Cor 1:31; 2 Cor 10:17). The only genuine attitude of the Christian in every age is the unfailing recognition of God's omnipresent gifts. The Christian prayer par excellence is "Thanks be to God for his inexpressible gift!" (2 Cor 9:15).

4:8 Already you are filled! Already you have become rich! Without us you have become kings! And would that you did reign, so that we might share the rule with you! Like all genuine lovers, like all dedicated ministers, Paul is deeply concerned about the attitude of some Corinthians. Comprehensible though their hubris be, it still remains contrary to all he has just reminded them of: "What have you that you did not receive? If then you received it, why do you boast as if it were not a gift?" Nothing is easier than to imagine the gift as mine by right, to divorce the gift from the giver. The urge is almost irresistible, both to boast of the gift as if it were a personal possession and to flaunt it as a challenge to those we deem to be less favorably endowed.

In the work of the ministry, little can surprise us in the attitude of the Corinthians and their sisters and brothers down the ages. The twofold temptation is in evidence throughout history: either to exaggerate the status of the minister beyond all reason ("I am for Paul," "I am for Apollos," and so on); or else, having once glimpsed "the light of the gospel" (2 Cor 4:4), to despise the minister as an incult hobbledehoy, defective in intelligence, and ill equipped to guide the wise of the world in their newfound wisdom.

4:9 For I think that God has exhibited us apostles as last of all, like men sentenced to death; because we have become a spectacle to the world, to angels and to men. In writing these words, the apostle to the Corinthians acknowledges no more than the truth of his situation and that of any other genuine apostle in every age. That the verse strikes us as odd, perhaps even hard to comprehend, is due to the alteration that has taken place in the apostolic status over the centuries. The irony of the previous verse (4:8) is irony no more. The apostle is king, does reign, wields his rule, and has turned the service of apostleship into a genuine spectacle "to world, to angels and to men." Men traverse seas, cross continents, pay dearly for the privilege of seeing Paul's concept of apostleship stood on its head. But, even at the other extreme of the scale, when an apostle most resembles "men sentenced to death," the spectacle is more irresistible still. Nothing pleases the world more than to march in the funeral procession of what seemed immortal.

4:10 We are fools for Christ's sake, but you are wise in Christ. We are weak, but you are strong. You are held in honor, but we in disrepute. Many commentators regard verses 10–13 as irony. They are not. Their implication cannot be that easily sidestepped. What Paul says here is but a variation on the theme "For the wisdom of this world is folly with God" (1 Cor 3:19) and its obverse. He goes on to add:

4:11–13 To the present hour we hunger and thirst, we are ill-clad and buffeted and homeless, and we labor, working with our own hands. Strange though it may sound, this need not be an inaccurate or an exaggerated picture of the apostolate. After all, "a disciple is not above his teacher, nor a servant above his master; it is enough for the disciple to be like his teacher, and the servant like his master. If they have called the master of the house Beelzebul, how much more will they malign those of his household" (Matt 10:24–25). If the master was maligned, if he had "nowhere to lay his head" (Matt 8:20; Luke 9:58), why should the servant (or "slave" as the Greek has it) be any better? The only difficult thing to comprehend is how the servants have so often managed to avoid the hardships and inconveniences.

Even a hasty reading of Second Corinthians will bear out the truth of what Paul says here. His lot is no better than his master's. He leads a life "through great endurance, in afflictions, hardships, calamities," labors, imprisonments, countless beatings, shipwreck, toil and hardship, sleepless nights, hunger and thirst, cold and exposure. "And, apart from other things, there is the daily pressure upon me of my anxiety for all the churches" (2 Cor 6:4; 11:23–29). He can sum up his attitude thus: "For the sake of Christ, then, I am content with weaknesses, insults, hardships, persecutions, and calamities; for when I am weak, then I am strong" (2 Cor 12:10). Ministers of the community were never meant to devote "the time they could spare from the feathering of

First Corinthians 4

their nests to the denial of their vocation." Of course, Ezekiel 34:1–11 puts it more bluntly still:

> The word of the Lord came to me: "Son of man, proph-
> esy against the shepherds of Israel, prophesy, and say to
> them, even to the shepherds, Thus says the Lord God:
> Ho, shepherds of Israel who have been feeding your-
> selves! Should not shepherds feed the sheep? You eat the
> fat, you clothe yourselves with the wool, you slaughter
> the fatlings; but you do not feed the sheep. The weak you
> have not strengthened, the sick you have not healed, the
> crippled you have not bound up, the strayed you have not
> brought back, the lost you have not sought, and with
> force and harshness you have ruled them. So they were
> scattered, because there was no shepherd; and they
> became food for all the wild beasts. My sheep were scat-
> tered, they wandered over all the mountains and on every
> high hill; my sheep were scattered over all the face of the
> earth, with none to search or seek for them. Therefore,
> you shepherds, hear the word of the Lord: As I live, says
> the Lord God, because my sheep have become a prey,
> and my sheep have become food for all the wild beasts,
> since there was no shepherd; and because my shepherds
> have not searched for my sheep, but the shepherds have
> fed themselves, and have not fed my sheep; therefore,
> you shepherds, hear the word of the Lord: Thus says the
> Lord God, Behold, I am against the shepherds; and I will
> require my sheep at their hand, and put a stop to their
> feeding the sheep; no longer shall the shepherds feed
> themselves. I will rescue my sheep from their mouths,
> that they may not be food for them. For thus says the
> Lord God: Behold, I, I myself will search for my sheep,
> and will seek them out."

*When reviled, we bless; when persecuted, we endure; when slan-
dered, we try to conciliate; we have become, and are now, as the*

refuse of the world, the offscouring of all things. These words echo the admirable portrait of the true apostle in 2 Corinthians 4:8–10. Here the accumulated details climax in "the refuse of the world, the offscouring of all things." The temptation is to assign such traits of the apostolate exclusively to the age of martyrs, when, as Saint Irenaeus says, the voice of the apostles was still audible. Having been for too long "in love with easeful" life, we are likely to think the portrait Paul draws is no more than an archaic curiosity. Nevertheless, a moment's reflection will show today's Christian communities in many quarters reviled, persecuted, and slandered. Where, then, is their "blessing" of those who revile them? What evidence of "endurance" is there before the onslaught of persecution, albeit a subtle, socially sanitized, and politically sanctioned "democratic" persecution? Where is there any indication of the churches' attempts to conciliate, save in devious and underhanded ways, when slandered?

4:14 I do not write this to make you ashamed, but to admonish you as my beloved children. Paul's disclaimer is easy enough to comprehend. His attitude to the Corinthians is no less in evidence in his dealings with the other churches: "But we were gentle among you, like a nurse taking care of her children" (1 Thess 2:7); "You know how, like a father with his children, we exhorted each one of you and encouraged you and charged you" (2:11); "For you are our glory and joy" (2:20); and "For God is my witness, how I yearn for you all with the affection of Christ Jesus" (Phil 1:8).

Paul's care not to have the Corinthians take his words amiss is some indication of his attitude toward them. The content of First Corinthians is proof enough of his affectionate solicitude for that church. This attitude has been sometimes interpreted as paternalism, authoritarianism, or any other such ""ism," but only because the ideals of ministry—so aptly set forth by the apostle—have been misunderstood.

4:15 For though you have countless guides in Christ, you do not have many fathers. For I became your father in Christ Jesus through the gospel. Unfashionable and politically incorrect though the expression may seem today, it remains nonetheless cogent and compelling. That the apostle begot the Corinthian believers "through the gospel" is precisely what establishes the bond of love, service, and respect between the minister and the community. Should this simple truth prove hard to accept, it is because the ministry in the church has been transformed into the image of a worldly profession, a trade. Apprenticeship in it, far from being a study of 1 Corinthians 4:11–13, is merely the gleaning of psychological techniques and sociological jargon, the acquisition of dubious theological aphorisms and questionable moral premises.

Consign Paul's caring attitude to the attic of ancient curiosities, and today's litany of abuses in the church seems more than understandable. To build a Christian community on any basis other than the gospel of Jesus Christ is to prepare a culture medium where all the ills of humanity pullulate.

4:16 I urge you, then, be imitators of me. Such a sentiment might surprise many, but it says no more than that the life of the preacher is as much a message as his words. Saint Augustine urges the Christian messenger to make the life he leads "the eloquence of his words." In this endeavor, as in no other, how the messenger lives is an integral part of the message she or he proclaims. In an altogether special sense, one can say the Word has to become flesh before it is either intelligible or credible.

To those disposed to criticize Paul at every turn, who see in this exhortation a blinding arrogance that set itself up as a model for imitation, one need only recall what "Be imitators of me" here entails. Be imitators of one who knew "much affliction and anguish of heart" (2 Cor 2:4)? Of one who has gone "through great endurance, in afflictions, hardships, calamities, beatings, imprisonments, tumults, labors, watching, hunger" (2 Cor 6:4–5; see 11:23–27)? If this be the stuff of pride and egotism, then let us have more of it.

4:17 Therefore I sent to you Timothy, my beloved and faithful child in the Lord, to remind you of my ways in Christ, as I teach them everywhere in every church. The bond of affection that binds Paul to his congregation is all the stronger and more intimate with his fellow workers. His title to paternity by reason of the gospel he preached to the Corinthians (1 Cor 4:14–15) is even more compelling when an individual like Timothy, who is Paul's right hand, is concerned. Collaborative ministry preaches the gospel no less in the bond of love that binds the ministers than in the message they proclaim. The two adjectives Paul uses to describe his "child in the Lord," *beloved* and *faithful*, sum up admirably the ideal of collaborative ministry in every age.

Having been proselytized and converted to the faith, the community of believers is never, or ought never to be, abandoned to its own devices. Christian communities of believers, even after two millennia, are in constant need of a reminder of the gospel they confess. Ministry in the Christian community is not a luxury but a compelling need. The onslaught of the world and its ways of thought and life are incessant, and so must the reminder of the truth of the gospel be. Timothy and his epigones through the centuries are not there to purvey novelties of dogma or to advance new revelations but to "remind" the believers of what has been and continues to be the gospel of Jesus Christ, always and everywhere "in every church."

4:18 *Some are arrogant, as though I were not coming to you.* "Arrogant" is so broad in its implications that it could mislead. Some Corinthians, confident they are not going to see Paul again, are "puffed up" with their self-importance and, doubtless, with the cleverness of their inventions and ideas. The phenomenon is but a facet of the wisdom syndrome in Corinth. Mistaking the wisdom of the gospel for the popular item of the same name, they set out to chart their own course to self-aggrandizement, exploiting the good news for the satisfaction of personal aspirations, theirs and their fellow Christians'. This is not a case of the mice playing in the absence of the cat. It is rather like children running riot in the absence of their teacher. First Corinthians furnishes sundry examples of just such behavior.

4:19 But I will come to you soon, if the Lord wills, and I will find out not the talk of these arrogant people but their power. This is not a threat but a promise. Paul really intends to visit them "if the Lord wills." The godless equivalent of the phrase today is the catachrestic "hopefully." But, however unpopular such expressions as "God willing," "please God," "with God's help" have become, they are part of the Christian idiom of civility from the very beginning. Indeed, the phrase is called the *conditio Iacobaea*, because we find its classic formulation enjoined in that manual of Christian etiquette, James 4:14–15, "Whereas you do not know about tomorrow...you ought to say, '*If the Lord wills*, we shall live and we shall do this or that.'"

Paul's use of the "Jacobean proviso" was prescient. As things turned out, he was prevented from making his promised visit for a good while, and that set off all the problems that necessitated the painful correspondence we possess in Second Corinthians. Nevertheless, the rest of First Corinthians provides ample opportunities to put both the "talk" and the "power" of "these arrogant people" on display.

4:20 For the kingdom of God does not consist in talk but in power. How readily the truth of this affirmation has been either caricatured or vitiated! The first thing to hold firmly is that the kingdom, the reign, the sovereignty, is God's and no one else's. The documents of more recent times, in Vatican I and II, about the relation of the phrase to the church, are only the latest phase of the ongoing debate. The power of which the kingdom of God consists is, of course, none other than the Holy Spirit. The gospel in every age is proclaimed "not only in word, but also in power and in the Holy Spirit" (1 Thess 1:5). How readily this power has been confounded with the might of the strong in the world and their arms of coercion, is, alas, a recurrent theme in the history of the church.

4:21 What do you wish? Shall I come to you with a rod, or with love in a spirit of gentleness? How admirably Paul modulates his tone in writing to the Corinthians. They might choose to act as children, but the "rod" is not what they require. All the force of the final rhetorical question is in the reaffirmation of the "love" and "the spirit of gentleness" that mark, or ought to mark, Christian ministry from the first century to the last.

Chapter 5

FIRST CORINTHIANS 5

5:1 It is actually reported that there is sexual immorality [NRSV] among you,... Two principal sources of information about Corinth were available to Paul: oral reports and written correspondence. This particular problem of "sexual immorality"—the RSV's "immorality" is too general to be adequate here, because there are many ways of being immoral other than the sexual—reached the apostle by word of mouth, from people who had traveled from Corinth to, in all likelihood, Ephesus, where Paul happened to be.

and of a kind that is not found even among pagans; for a man is living with his father's wife. The sexual immorality brought to Paul's attention was of a kind not tolerated even in the reputedly dissolute atmosphere of Corinth. The prevalent permissiveness of a pagan society like Corinth's drew the line at the violation of family bonds. Under Augustus Caesar, severe laws were enacted to safeguard the probity of the family: laws against adultery (the *lex Iulia de adulteriis*) and for the institution of marriage (the *lex Iulia maritandis ordinibus*). It is so easy to forget that Corinth lay within the extensive bounds of the Roman Empire. It is more difficult to imagine any reader of Paul's epistles at the time who was not within the confines of that empire.

The enormity reported to Paul involved a man and his stepmother, "his father's wife." If the fact itself, however rare (?) in modern societies, surprises us, delating sexual misdemeanors to the authorities must be thoroughly familiar to us. Amid the clamor and protest of the shocked citizens, whether in Corinth or in any of our cities, Paul's astonished reaction ought to be thoroughly comprehensible. Yet, herein lies a problem. So ready are we to understand the situation that we fail to see its real essence in these verses (5:1–4).

5:2 And you are arrogant! Ought you not rather to mourn? Let him who has done this be removed from among you. Paul's astonishment at the "arrogance" of the Corinthians must give us pause. Whatever the reaction of a society to such an event, it certainly cannot be arrogance. If nothing else, hypocrisy should see to that. Were the deed confined to a sex act, however perverse or taboo, the reaction of its witnesses could scarcely be pride or arrogance.

Paul, moreover, calls for the removal of "him who has done this" from the community. But this individual's sexual misdemeanor was not solitary. It involved a partner, his father's wife, and yet there is no mention of removing her from the community. Surely, this cannot be chalked up to Paul's "feminism" *avant la lettre*.

5:3 For though absent in body I am present in spirit, and as if present, I have already pronounced judgment... There is no doubt in the apostle's mind about what needs to be done. But, unlike most of his successors, he does not interfere with the workings and decisions of the community. If there is instruction to be given, he is duty bound to give it, and he does give it clearly and succinctly. If there is a problem to be tackled, then the community must tackle it, in the light of the gospel he preached to them. The apostle's task is to alleviate their ignorance, not to supplant their power of decision. So accustomed are we to direct intervention into the local affairs of the tiniest of congregations by higher authorities that we need to reflect long and deeply on Paul's example. As he explains in his letter to Philemon, "I preferred to do nothing without your consent in order that your goodness might not be by compulsion but of your own free will" (Phlm 14).

5:4 in the name of the Lord Jesus on the man who has done such a thing. One of the unfortunate disadvantages of verse divisions in the New Testament is its arbitrariness. Verses 3 and 4 evidently belong together, and the break, where it is at present, is misplaced and misleading. Moreover, several years ago, Father Jerome Murphy-O'Connor drew attention to an unjustified alteration of the word order in the Greek text of these two verses. Upon closer inspection of the Greek original, and disregarding the arbitrary comma, one ought to read the verses thus:

> I have already pronounced judgment on the man *who has done such a thing in the name of the Lord Jesus.*

This verse, sadly, can be misused to legitimate abuse of ecclesiastical authority. Paul does not pass judgment on the sexual aberration. That would be redundant at best. If the Corinthians failed to see the evil in the act, they had to be indeed severely immature children. There was no need for Paul to add his condemnation to what pagan society itself would not tolerate, "sexual immorality...of a kind that is not found even among pagans" (1 Cor 5:1).

The problem Paul has to confront is an aberration not in sexual mores but in the understanding of the gospel. The culprit's deed was perpetrated as part of his misinterpretation of the new-found freedom in Christ Jesus, an egregious misreading of "There is therefore now no condemnation for those who are in Christ Jesus" (Rom 8:1). There were in Corinth two opposing attitudes for what the redemption in Christ Jesus meant: one ascetic, to which we will come shortly; and the other libertine, a sample of which we have here. Having been redeemed by Christ, the man in this instance argues, and his fellow Corinthians concur—which is why they are arrogant—that the Christian converts need no longer be bound by all the old restraints that formerly governed their actions. The man's action was thus the reason for boasting, and for the arrogance of those who approved it. We must not forget that someone from that community brought the situation to Paul's attention and was, therefore, not among the arrogant.

This reading of the text, by the way, is the explanation why the man's sexual partner does not figure in the indictment. To opine, without any evidence either way, that she was not a Christian and hence not subject to Paul's authority is to forget that Paul here explicitly refrains from applying his authority even to the Christian members of the community.

When you are assembled, and my spirit is present, with the power of our Lord Jesus,... Keeping in mind that the problem here has to do with the proper understanding of the given of the faith, several conditions are laid down by Paul. First of all, it has to be the decision of the community itself, "when you are assembled." Then, having made his own position clear—"I have already pronounced judgment" (1 Cor 5:3)—he expects them to be mindful of his teaching—"My spirit is present." Finally, and most important of all, their decision is to be taken "with the power of our Lord Jesus," as much as to say, with the aid of the Holy Spirit. This, by the way, is still a valid procedure for any Christian community. Commenting on Matthew 16:15–18, Saint Augustine preaches in a sermon, "For it was not one man who received the keys, but the entire Church considered as one." Relegating such responsibility to an individual, or to a few, is a dereliction of duty.

5:5 you are to deliver this man to Satan for the destruction of the flesh, that his spirit may be saved in the day of the Lord [Jesus]. Before all else, I need to confess, together with many other and far better interpreters of Paul, my ignorance of the meaning of this verse, but not, however, without calling attention to an important point: the punishment envisaged is certainly not eternal damnation, because its ultimate purpose is the salvation of the individual concerned "in the day of the Lord." Readings in the history of the church in any century will yield rich examples of how these obscure verses in First Corinthians have been grossly misinterpreted and misapplied. They confirm that a small error in the beginning inevitably leads to enormities in the end.

5:6 Your boasting is not good. Do you not know that a little leaven leavens the whole lump? To boast, to be arrogant, about such a reading of the gospel message is simply "not good." The truism of the second part of the verse is a warning about how readily faith aberrations can and do spread in any community. A brief reflection on the verse itself should suffice to convince us that the problem here is not primarily sexual. To apply the leaven image to sexual conduct is not quite appropriate.

5:7 *Cleanse out the old leaven that you may be a new lump, as you really are unleavened.* The pagan background of many in Corinth takes time to be "cleansed." Conversion to Christianity does not rid you overnight of the prejudices and presuppositions with which you come into the faith. Doubtless, just such a background in paganism led the man in question, as well as other Corinthians, to their arrogance (5:2). Time, in its slow infinitude, is needed to allow the "new lump" to become what Paul will call "the unleavened bread of sincerity and truth."

For Christ, our paschal lamb, has been sacrificed. How admirably, and with what economy, is the image of God's holy people in the exodus evoked (Exod 12:21–27)! Paul, "of the people of Israel…a Hebrew born of Hebrews," knows only too well the Passover tradition. As a follower of Christ, he sees the fulfillment of that event in the person of Jesus. This is a method of reading Scripture allegorically, seeing the persons or events of the Old Testament (Adam, crossing the sea, the manna) as "types" (Rom 5:14) that find their fulfillment in the New Testament as "anti-types" (Christ, baptism, Eucharist). Nevertheless, as we shall see in 1 Corinthians 11, Paul, although aware of all this, will, unlike the Synoptics (Luke 22:15), make no reference to the Passover in the institution account of the Eucharist.

5:8 *Let us, therefore, celebrate the festival, not with the old leaven, the leaven of malice and evil, but with the unleavened bread of sincerity and truth.* The Passover imagery of cleansing the home of all the "old leaven" is here used to exhort the Christians to be rid of the old ways of "malice and evil" and to manifest their newness of life in "sincerity and truth." Nor is this a mirthless and lugubrious process of asceticism and penance. The key word in the new Christian life is *Celebrate*! Many Christians unfortunately have been more quick to mourn and be sad than to be glad and celebrate.

5:9 I wrote to you in my letter not to associate with sexually immoral [NRSV] men;... This is the first hint we have of a prior letter of Paul to the Corinthians. There have been, as is to be expected, endless attempts to find traces of the prior letter. But the simple fact of the matter is that we have no idea whatsoever what happened to it or why it was not preserved. One could at best guess that it was more than a brief note simply from the remark quoted here by Paul. Except in spy thrillers, you do not expect to find telegraphic style communications, for example, "Don't associate with sexually immoral men."

5:10 not at all meaning the immoral of this world, or the greedy and robbers, or idolaters, since then you would need to go out of the world. Nevertheless, it seems that in that lost letter this particular exhortation ran the risk of being misunderstood. So Paul tries, in First Corinthians, to correct the misapprehension. Understandable though the misconstruing of the remark be, Paul's correction is down-to-earth common sense. The world being what it is, no Christian can be expected to avoid all dealings with it. Even the anchorites of the Egyptian desert in the early centuries had some dealings with the world. Paul is a realist; he wants his fellow Christians to be realists too.

The presupposition of Paul's assertion is, obviously, the expectation that Christians themselves, even in this "evil and adulterous generation" (Matt 16:4), ought to shun immorality, greed, thievery, idolatry, and the like. This conflict between the life they must lead and the world in which they must lead it in is at the basis of many of the problems that arose in Corinth and have continued to arise in Christian communities to our day. Being a

Christian is an onerous task because it has to take place in the midst of a hostile and uncomprehending world.

5:11 But rather I wrote to you not to associate with any one who bears the name of brother if he is guilty of immorality or greed, or is an idolater, reviler, drunkard, or robber—not even to eat with such a one. This is the stuff that feeds the current anti-Paul sentiment. Here's a bigot, judgmental, arbitrary, tyrannical, and all the litany of defamatory adjectives. The rebuttals to each category mentioned by Paul come tripping off the tongue: Hasn't he heard of market economy? Of alcoholism as disease? Of pluralism? Of the right of the poor not to starve?

Was there ever a time in history when this verse was not applied literally, without regard for its original context? But, before leaping to unwarranted conclusions, one must consider the situation in Corinth at the time. Without letting the imagination run wild, think of the community of believers: a small number of converts to a new faith living in a metropolis teeming with different religions and cults, ingenious in offering a diversity of pleasures and convenient paths to salvation. A community of ethnically diversified populations in all walks of life, from the most louche to the loftiest. Before condemning Paul, one should honestly try to devise some means of protecting the integrity of the small, timorous, despised band of believers in that situation.

5:12 For what have I to do with judging outsiders? Is it not those inside the church whom you are to judge? The task of judging those outside the church is not ours. This does not mean that we are unaware of their reprehensible actions or are incapable of calling their genuine evil by its name. The Christian community's concern is with those who are inside the church. The judgment, when it is called for, can be directed to them and to no one else. The community has the obligation to be ever-vigilant to safeguard the integrity and holiness of its members. The New Testament even provides a sample of such procedure (Matt 18:15–17).

5:13 *God judges those outside. "Drive out the wicked person from among you."* God is the ultimate judge, and the judgment of "those outside" belongs exclusively to him. The grave confusion resulting from the concluding verses of this chapter (5:9–13) arises out of the fact that, once Christianity was in the majority anywhere, Christian leaders sometimes arrogated to themselves the divine prerogatives. They not only trespassed the limits of their jurisdiction with regard to outsiders, but they also invaded the rights and privileges of their fellow Christians in the community. The Deuteronomic injunction, "So you shall purge the evil from the midst of you" (Deut 17:7), has always invited aberrant interpretations.

Chapter 6

FIRST CORINTHIANS 6

6:1 When one of you has a grievance against a brother, does he dare go to law before the unrighteous instead of the saints? Despite the evidently altered situation between then and now, these verses (6:1–8) are of the utmost relevance today. Going to law "before the unrighteous" in Corinth meant going to secular judges, to "unbelievers." Going to law today means, even in so-called Christian countries, going to a secular or secularized court. It was, moreover, much easier to go to "the saints," that is, to members of the Christian community (1 Cor 1:2; 14:33) in Corinth, than it is today; for the members of the community are themselves, more often than not, more unrighteous than anything Corinth could have provided.

6:2 Do you not know that the saints will judge the world? And if the world is to be judged by you, are you incompetent to try trivial cases? Eschatology, the end of all things, is never far from Paul's mind, as it ought not to be from any believer's. Moreover, rhetorician that he is, he has recourse to a well-known type of argument, *a majore ad minus,* from the greater to the lesser. The prerogative of judgment, "You who have followed me will also sit on twelve thrones, judging the twelve tribes of Israel," is not an invention of Paul's. Now, if the faithful will exercise that type of solemn judgment, "when the Son of man shall sit on his glorious throne" (Matt 19:28), they are certainly amply competent to arbitrate "trivial cases." Of course, all cases, by comparison with the final assize, must seem trivial. The point to keep in mind is that Christians can and should resolve their problems without recourse to the unrighteous, the world.

6:3 Do you not know that we are to judge angels? How much more, matters pertaining to this life! Paul reiterates the same type of argument, raising the competence to judge the world to that of judging even the angels, the splendid creatures of the heavenly court. Their concerns are those of eternity, and their judgment of such matters far exceeds that of "matters pertaining to this life."

6:4 If then you have such cases, why do you lay them before those who are least esteemed by the church? The Corinthians indeed had such cases, and so do we in every age. What has radically altered, however, is that those who were "least esteemed by the church" of Corinth are today the most esteemed, revered, and honored by today's churches. The hopeless obliteration of the lines of demarcation today between the church and those least esteemed by it render the discussion of verses like these extremely difficult.

6:5 I say this to your shame. Can it be that there is no man among you wise enough to decide between members of the brotherhood,... What the Corinthians are doing is shameful, and Paul, true minister that he is, does not try to make light of the situation. In like situations, euphemisms would only aggravate the problem. What he says is "to their shame" simply because it is astonishing that the Christian community in Corinth failed to find someone "wise enough," and that in a city that prided itself on wisdom, to arbitrate matters not between strangers but between a band of brothers.

6:6 but brother goes to law against brother, and that before unbelievers? In a society as litigious as ours, this verse scarcely needs comment. What it needs, indeed, what it has needed all along, is to have the believers reflect upon it and judge their own actions unequivocally.

6:7 To have lawsuits at all with one another is defeat for you. Why not rather suffer wrong? Why not rather be defrauded? To modern ears this counsel has an archaic ring to it. The words seem like an utterance in a foreign tongue to a now-vanished people. Yet, it is hard to imagine how, in this matter, today's Christians differ from Corinth's. Is it perhaps that today we are the ones who do wrong to others and defraud them? Even prescinding from the evil we do, who in the Christian community is willing to consider that merely having lawsuits is a blemish, a marked defect, a "failure"? Not only do we have lawsuits, but we wish to exact the last farthing and wreak the direst penalty on any one who dares cross our path. Indeed, whenever any evil befalls us, we have become accustomed to seek any neighbor we can find to exact justice, in ingeniously varied unjust ways.

6:8 *But you yourselves wrong and defraud, and that even your own brethren.* The Christians in Corinth are, after all, more like us than we wish to acknowledge. Then as now "brother goes to law against brother" (6:6). That the Corinthians did so "before unbelievers" is no more distinctive of their situation than it is of ours. Hanging crucifixes in courtrooms is no more indicative of the faith than the blind scales are a guarantee of justice.

Reflection upon these verses (6:1–8) would offer a salutary reminder of how far we are from being what we claim or what we are called to be. Is the agenda of Christian rhetoric today a means of closing our eyes to more basic defects in our Christian society? Do we discourse volubly on the sins and crimes of others in order to drown out the truth of Paul's words?

6:9–10 *Do you not know that the unrighteous will not inherit the kingdom of God?* The question form is merely to stress what must be common knowledge for every believer, a self-evident truth. It is, as it were, a truism, that the unrighteous do not inherit the kingdom of God. To do that, you need to be children of God, "members of the household of God" (Eph 2:19), "heirs of God and fellow heirs with Christ" (Rom 8:17).

Do not be deceived; neither fornicators [NRSV], nor idolaters, nor adulterers, nor sexual perverts [NRSV: male prostitutes, sodomites], nor thieves, nor the greedy, nor drunkards, nor revilers, nor robbers will inherit the kingdom of God. Paul descends from the general unrighteous to the particular in order to explain his meaning. To do so, he has recourse to a common rhetorical device, a "list of vices" (a calque on the German *Lasterkataloge*). But, before getting bogged down by the individual items in this list, we do well to look at the very many similar lists in the New Testament (1 Cor 5:9–13; Rom 1:29–31; 13:13; 2 Cor 12:20–21; Gal 5:19–21; Eph 5:5; Mark 7:21–22, and on and on). Thus, in addition to the items in the list in 1 Corinthians 6, we have quarreling, jealousy, anger, selfishness, slander, gossip, conceit, disorder, impurity, licentiousness, idolatry, sorcery, enmity, strife, dissension, party spirit, envy, carousing, covetousness, evil thoughts, theft, murder, deceit, slander, pride, foolishness, and, as Galatians adds at the end of its very long list, "and things like these" (Gal 5:21 NRSV).

These lists must qualify among the most misunderstood and abused in the whole New Testament. If you must have recourse to them for whatever reason, you must keep in mind:

1. They are not a supplement to the Ten Commandments, nor an explication of them.
2. They are not exhaustive (see "and things like these" and "those who do such things" in Galatians 5:21).
3. They are not, strictly speaking, interdictions but rather negative descriptions of holiness: what a holy community (1 Cor 1:2; 6:11) eschews, refuses to countenance, let alone be arrogant about (5:2).
4. Despite the misnomer of the list ("of vices" for the German *Lasterkataloge*), the items in them are most emphatically not seen as vices and virtues in any Scholastic acceptation of the terms. The lists are not, in other words, commentaries on Aristotle's *Nichomachean Ethics* nor the bases for Saint Thomas's second part of *The Summa Theologica*. They are not components of a moral theology.

It follows, therefore, that, under no circumstances should you:

1. Operate a triage among them, picking and choosing what offends your sensibilities, your national prejudices, or your racial bias, or
2. Establish a hierarchy among them, deciding, for example, that greed and drunkenness are not on the same footing as fornication and adultery or in the same category as slander or foolishness, or
3. Use them as cases of conscience, or cite them as a moral code, in any sense, in whatever century, whether the first or the twenty-first.

6:11 And such were some of you. But you were washed, you were sanctified, you were justified in the name of the Lord Jesus Christ and in the Spirit of our God. This is the whole crux of the matter. The Corinthians, prior to their conversion, were once all these things mentioned in verses 9 and 10. Now that they are the "new creation" (2 Cor 5:17), they must shrink in horror from all such demeanor. They are no longer unrighteous. They belong to the household of God and must act and live accordingly. This is what these lists are all about: Become what you are, people who have been cleansed, sanctified, and made righteous ("justified") in the name of the Lord Jesus Christ. After all, *noblesse oblige!* One can rightly wonder what the Christian community would be like today had this gospel been preached to them rather than the endless indictments against this or that select item in the lists.

6:12 "All things are lawful for me," but not all things are helpful [NRSV: beneficial]. Yet another trait that binds the Corinthians to us is their love of slogans. Like those of our times, their slogans embraced a wide spectrum of views, even the most contradictory. This particular slogan, "All things are lawful for me" (another modern English version has "I am free to do anything"), is within the ambit of Christian freedom and its consequences. In all likelihood, the man living with his father's wife (5:1) adopted such a slogan.

Paul never denies the truth of the statement. But he distinguishes it by specifying that "not all things are useful [beneficial]." In other words, the exercise of Christian freedom must be defined by its limits and—as we shall have occasion to see in 1 Corinthians 8—this limit is the other, the neighbor, the brother. Freedom is a gift we have in Christ Jesus: "our freedom which we have in Christ Jesus" (Gal 2:4); and, like all gifts, it brings with it responsibility. In this instance, the exercise of the gift of freedom is not absolute but conditioned by the need of the other in the community. The eponymous hero of Albert Camus's *Caligula* remarks that one is always free at somebody else's expense. That Christians are often reckless in the practice of their freedom is not the triumph of a Corinthian slogan but the misunderstanding of a gift.

"All things are lawful for me," but I will not be enslaved by anything. Once again the repeated slogan is not denied but qualified. The qualification here arises not out of those affected by the exercise of the gift but out of the nature of the gift itself. To be genuinely free, one must be free from every created thing. For Paul, genuine freedom is always a freedom under God, a freedom that has the Lord for its sole master. To let my gift of freedom enslave me to any creature, even the holiest, is not to be free but enslaved and dominated by that thing. Paradoxical though it seems, to be enslaved by the slogan itself, "All things are lawful," is not to be free but to be in thrall to a dictum, however sublime.

The Christian, whether in Corinth or here today, must jealously guard this gift of freedom: "For freedom Christ has set us free" (Gal 5:1a), both in exercising it responsibly vis-à-vis the other and in guarding against its loss by enslavement to anyone or anything. "Stand fast therefore, and do not submit again to a yoke of slavery" (Gal 5:1b).

6:13 "Food is meant for the stomach and the stomach for food"— and God will destroy both one and the other. If the transition seems abrupt, it is simply that Paul passes on to a concrete application without further ado. Both the food and the stomach are creatures.

As such, they are mutable and perishable. A moment's reflection should suffice to show us how, in our own age, both food and the stomach can hinder the very freedom we have in Christ Jesus. In a homily commenting on Psalm 140:1, Augustine reminded his people, "Before God can liberate you, you must set yourself free."

The body is not meant for immorality [porneia, NRSV: fornication], but for the Lord, and the Lord for the body. This further example is more ponderous. Most people reading this verse will perhaps concentrate on its first part, "The body is not meant for immorality/ fornication," either to qualify it somehow or to dispute it outright. The fact of the matter is that the body is for the Lord, that is, is holy. This is simply the consequence of the Lord being for the body, having given himself up for us (Gal 2:20). As food and the cares of our stomach could deprive us of our freedom, so too fornication and preoccupation with our sex lives could reduce us to slavery.

6:14 And God raised the Lord and will also raise us up by his power. A famous commentary on First Corinthians bears the title *The Resurrection of the Dead.* The resurrection, the bodily resurrection, is most assuredly the horizon that defines this letter. The argument against sexual license is grounded in the given of the faith, that the body belongs to the Lord. It is further bolstered by the fact that this body is destined for resurrection. This given of the faith not only alters all the parameters of our self-understanding but also defines all our relationships. It was remarked earlier that much in this epistle is based on the sanctity of the elect (1 Cor 1:2; 6:11) everywhere. This verse simply reiterates this truth, namely, their sanctity by reason of their belonging to the Lord and their being destined for the resurrection.

6:15 Do you not know that your bodies are members of Christ? Once again, "Do you not know?" is a reminder of a fundamental truth of the faith (1 Cor 3:16; 5:6; 6:2, 3, 9, 15, 16, 19; 9:13, 24). That our bodies are "members of Christ" is not a metaphor. We *are* in fact members of Christ, not *like* members of Christ: "Now you are the body of Christ and individually members of it" (1 Cor 12:27).

One would have thought that this fact in and by itself ought to suffice to put paid to the endless debates and criticisms of the teaching of the church on chastity. Alas, the point of departure for Paul's position is the gospel (1 Cor 15:3–5).

Shall I therefore take the members of Christ and make them members of a prostitute [Greek: porne]? Never! The image is, evidently, hyperbolic. Its import, nevertheless, is clear. Paul takes seriously indeed our membership in the Body of Christ, the prime consequence of which membership is the inviolable sanctity of the person. What Christian believer, made aware of this status of sanctity, would be willing to trample it into the mire, not merely of sexual congress but of any deed that soils and defaces it? Mention was made earlier of *noblesse oblige*. Should not Christians be made aware repeatedly and continually of the nobility of their status as children of God and as members of the Body of Christ?

6:16 Do you not know that he who joins himself to a prostitute [Greek: porne] becomes one body with her? For, as it is written, "The two shall become one flesh." Paul gets carried away by the vehemence of his argument and even more by the ardor of his conviction. What at face value is a rhetorical question is not one at all. What is presumed as self-evident truth ("Do you not know?") is not. You do not have to be a metaphysician to know that sexual union with a prostitute can never make you "one body with her." The scriptural citation of Genesis 2:24, one of the more frequently quoted Old Testament passages in the New (Matt 19:5; Mark 10:7; Eph 5:31), is about marriage between man and woman, that is, between two persons, not between a person and a hired object, as Paul says here.

6:17 But he who is united to the Lord becomes one spirit with him. A good example of a non sequitur in the argument. Rather than pursue the inaccurate line of reasoning in the previous verse, Paul returns to the solid ground of incontrovertible truth. Union with the Lord means not only living out of the same spirit, but seeing and judging with the same mind: "Have this mind among yourselves, which is yours in Christ Jesus" (Phil 2:5).

6:18 Shun immorality [porneia, NRSV: fornication]. Every other sin which a man commits is outside the body; but the immoral man [porneuōn, NRSV: the fornicator] *sins against his own body.* The main point of the passage (6:12–20), indeed of both chapters (1 Cor 5 and 6), can be summed up in "Shun immorality/fornication!" Before quitting the subject of sexual immorality in these last two chapters, however, it is necessary to remind ourselves that the term and its cognates, which are variously translated in the RSV, the NAB, and the NRSV as "immorality," "sexual immorality," "fornication," and so on, all render one Greek term and its cognates: *porneia* (whence we have, for example, the English "pornography"). The RSV consistently but inaccurately translates it "immorality." The NRSV flits between "sexual immorality" and "fornication" for no discernible reason, certainly not in the Greek text. The reader will be well advised to keep in mind the Greek *porneia* whenever the RSV, the NAB, or the NRSV employs any of the English equivalents.

The gravity of such immoral acts is that they involve the whole person. Augustine remarks somewhere that you can discuss philosophy at table, but not in bed. The sex act involves the whole person, and this is the reason why Paul adds that whoever commits *porneia* sins against his own body. The unexpressed thought here is that this body is a member of Christ. Of course, Paul is not slow to draw the conclusion that ought to serve as the inalterable principle of all Christian sexual conduct:

6:19 Do you not know that your body is a temple of the Holy Spirit within you, which you have from God? As one is readily led to believe from the "Do you not know?," this is an indisputable given of the gospel faith. You as a person, "your body" in biblical terminology, are a dwelling place of God's great gift to the believer: the Holy Spirit.

71

When Christians have such a basis for their holiness of life, one can rightly wonder why they need to have recourse to Aristotelian, Stoic, or Thomistic ethics to keep them on the straight and narrow. Why are its echoes so faint in Christian preaching and teaching?

You are not your own;... This is a corollary to the indwelling of the Holy Spirit in us. We are simply not our own; we do not belong to ourselves, whatever we choose to believe. The fact itself is all the more unpalatable in our world where everyone insists on her or his own right over their body. Has anyone ever stopped to question a Christian believer whence he or she came by such right? If they have not, perhaps it is because Christians have not been sufficiently reminded that the reason they are not their own is simply because they have been purchased at an infinite price (1 Cor 6:20; 7:23) and belong to some One else.

6:20 you were bought with a price. That price, of course, was "not with perishable things such as silver or gold, but with the precious blood of Christ" (1 Pet 1:18–19). Such a title to a Christian's dignity is not only reason for shunning all *porneia*, but it must be the rule in the believer's attitude and treatment of every other person she or he encounters. A little thought ought to suffice to convince us that this is an incontestable motive in dealing with the other, whoever she or he happens to be. How could one believe that the other, male or female, child or adult, stranger or familiar, everyone bought with the precious blood of Christ, can be made the object of *porneia* in any sense of the term?

So glorify God in your body. What other means has the Christian for glorifying God, for declaring to the world at large God's great gift, and bearing witness to the gratitude that is ours in the realization that this God made us temples of the Spirit of his Son? Paul does not add this exhortation idly. He knew whereof he spoke: "It is my eager expectation and hope that...now as always Christ will be honored in my body, whether by life or by death. For to me to live is Christ, and to die is gain" (Phil 1:20–21).

Chapter 7

FIRST CORINTHIANS 7

7:1 Now concerning the matters about which you wrote. It is well for a man not to touch a woman. Hitherto Paul has dealt with matters that came to his attention by word of mouth. Now he takes up questions addressed to him in a letter from the Corinthian community.

We have already seen among some Christians in Corinth a tendency to what might be called "libertinism," for example, the slogan, "All things are lawful for me" (6:12). Here we find the exact opposite tendency, what we might call the "ascetic," exemplified in the slogan, "It is well for a man not to touch a woman." Both tendencies have cropped up periodically in the history of Christianity. Although, over the centuries, the libertine tendency was quickly stifled, the ascetic tendency at times moved in unhealthy directions.

Once again, in dealing with this ascetic slogan, Paul does not deny it, but qualifies it. He does not deny that, even in marriage, it is good in general for a man or a woman not to have sex, legitimate though it be. This is why the slogan is characterized as "ascetic." It gives up a perfectly good thing in the name of some higher motive like prayer, or self-abnegation, or the like. To give up what is clearly a sin would hardly constitute an ascetic practice.

7:2 But because of the temptation to immorality [NRSV: the cases of sexual immorality], each man should have his own wife and each woman her own husband. Despite the two English versions, what the Greek text says is simply, "But because of *porneia*." Modern sophisticates are apt to think questionable or unworthy the reason Paul gives for marrying. The fact of the matter is simply that Paul

73

himself is incapable of conceiving coition of any kind outside marriage. This conviction is at the basis of all he has to say about sexual matters here. Incidentally, it is also at the basis of all that the church in past centuries has taught and continues to teach on sexual matters, however reluctant it seems at times to spell this out. The principle is and remains every bit as valid today for Christian believers as it was for Paul and the Corinthians. One might, for reasons of one's own, reject it out of hand, laugh to scorn those who hold it, or even legislate against it; but no one can refuse Paul and his fellow believers the right to hold it, defend it, and live by its truth, however antiquated.

7:3 The husband should give to his wife her conjugal rights, and likewise the wife to her husband. This might well be an instance of one of the spouses refusing "conjugal rights" to the other on the basis of the ascetic slogan. If to avoid *porneia* you get married, then you cannot very well display your ascetical heroism at your partner's expense.

The entire chapter 7, moreover, can serve as a perfect example of the evenhandedness with which Paul treats both males and females in the community. You will not find in the literature of the period anything remotely resembling the equity with which Paul deals out his advice in this most important aspect of the relationship between the sexes. It is all the more necessary to call attention to this trait of Paul's thought, if only to give the lie to the gratuitous charge of misogyny leveled against him.

7:4 For the wife does not rule over her own body, but the husband does; likewise the husband does not rule over his own body, but the wife does. It is far from untypical of the endemic misinterpretation of the Pauline writings to split this verse in two, conveniently obliterating its second part, and disregarding the crucial "likewise" altogether. The mutuality of subjection, most aptly summed up in that other misplaced and hence obliterated verse, "Be subject to one another out of reverence for Christ"(Eph 5:21), gives expression to the very essence of the bond that makes Christian marriage what it is.

All too often, readers forget that the verse in 1 Corinthians 7:4 only makes explicit what the previous verse had said about the reciprocal respect for the conjugal rights of the marriage partner. Such rights, moreover, are not subject to arbitration by unbelievers, those "who are least esteemed by the church" (6:6, 4), however mighty and esteemed in the eyes of the world.

7:5 Do not refuse one another except perhaps by agreement for a season, that you may devote yourselves to prayer; but then come together again, lest Satan tempt you through lack of self-control. Part of the realism that governs Paul's thinking in this matter is the day-to-day life of the Christian. In this verse he gives an admirable illustration of how the spouses rule over one another's body. How, in other words, the conjugal rights are in fact exercised. For this, Paul chooses the case of abstaining from conjugal intercourse. He sets three conditions:

1. Mutual agreement of the couple
2. for a specified length of time, and
3. at the end of that period, to come together again.

This means that one of the spouses cannot simply decide on her or his own to go on a thirty-day retreat. Nor, at the end of the period, can the partner be left on tenterhooks awaiting the indulgent pleasure of the retreatant. All this is in line with Paul's point of departure. If you cannot do without sex, then get married. The stranded spouse ought not to be abandoned to temptation while his or her partner sets off on the quest of Christian perfection.

7:6 I say this by way of concession, not of command. Paul's language is an example of authority being exercised with prudence and moderation, inviting assent rather than commanding it. In the community of believers, the rule of those in authority is a sacred and God-given trust. As Pope Paul VI noted in his Monte

Cassino retreat, "Authority in the church is a service, not an honor." The author of First Peter draws up an infrequently remembered portrait of this ecclesiastical authority:

> So I exhort the elders among you....Tend the flock of God that is your charge, not by constraint but willingly, not for shameful gain but eagerly, not as domineering over those in your charge but being examples to the flock. (1 Pet 5:1–3)

7:7 I wish that all were as I myself am. Nothing can be more natural than such an attitude. Often, however, we are all too ready to make of our natural proclivities and personal preferences expressions of the will of God. Almost from the earliest times, the believers were sorted into two major categories: first-class celibates and second-rate married folk. So many practices of Christian life had their origin in the desire of the less fortunate to have some small share in the singular good fortune of those who have left the world for the unmelanged bliss of the celibate life. A father of the church is said to have derived the etymology of *celibate* from the Latin *caeli beatus,* "heavenly bliss."

But each has his own special gift from God, one of one kind and one of another. Hard though it is to miss the meaning of these words, centuries of interpretation took them to mean that the celibate, chaste life was a charism, but married life was not. In the context of what Paul has said thus far, there is no escaping the fact that the husband–wife state is a charism "of one kind," and foregoing this state is also a charism "of another" kind. The words themselves, if they have any meaning at all, allow no one-sided interpretation such as has prevailed over the years.

Unlike many of those who came after him, Paul never thought that a life of celibate chastity can be demanded of everyone. Unless God has granted such a gift, it is futile to require it as a condition, for example, for the exercise of the ministry. It is important to remember that church authority is impotent to confer any charism of any sort on any individual. It can, at best, only recognize its existence in one or another.

A word on vocabulary usage here might not be amiss. The current popular term for abstinence from sexual activity is *celibacy*. This simply means the status of being "celibate," unmarried. The term for sexual abstinence, the term employed, for example, for religious vows, is *chastity*. Many married people live lives of exemplary chastity. And yet many celibate persons do not live lives of chastity. Pope Alexander VI, the Borgia pope, for instance, was celibate, but no one would have called him chaste. The confusion of these two terms is at the basis of a great deal of misunderstanding in the current discussion of sex in Christian life.

7:8 To the unmarried and the widows I say that it is well for them to remain single as I do. Throughout this chapter, the only alternative for an unmarried person who does not possess the charism of abstaining from sexual activity altogether is to get married (7:2), that is, to recognize that she or he not only lacks the gift of sexual abstinence but has the charism of marriage (7:7). Note, however, that Paul here is not laying down a rule. He knows he cannot in such matters, because only God allots the charism "of one kind and of another" to each individual. It is up to each individual to discern which. All that Paul does in this verse is repeat what he said in 7:7, "I wish that all were as I myself am." That, as he must have known only too well, was no more than a velleity.

7:9 But if they cannot exercise self-control, they should marry. For it is better to marry than to be aflame with passion. Nothing could be clearer for anyone who, like Paul, sees the exercise of sex within the Christian life confined exclusively to marriage. The recognition of one's inability to "exercise self-control" is, in fact, not that you lack one charism but that you possess another, a different charism. So, get married! The Christian life is not meant to be squandered either in sterile regrets and frustrations or in tilting against the unruly windmills of God-given urges and dispositions.

Paul proceeds systematically to deal with the Corinthians' queries. First, he takes up the case of the unmarried and the widows. He then turns his attention to what is by far the greater category of the married. This vast majority of God's holy people have rated relatively little attention by comparison with the tomes dedicated to those who vowed chastity and led celibate lives in monastic seclusion. One is hard pressed to conceive, for example, in the vast literature of the patristic period, any encomium of the married life. The one gem in that vast reliquary of Christian wisdom is Clement of Alexandria's, but its explicit language in treating Christian marriage doomed it to the decent obscurity of dead languages.

7:10–11 To the married I give charge, not I but the Lord,... It is admirable that Paul, who elsewhere insists on his authority to teach the community, is careful here to separate the Lord's authority from his own (1 Cor 7:7). In a question as weighty as this, expressing an opinion that goes counter to the practice of Jews and Gentiles alike, as is the prohibition of divorce, it is all the more necessary to insist on the authoritative source of the teaching, namely the Lord himself. It should be kept in mind, moreover, that the very use of the title "Lord" says more than "the Word of Jesus." It says, rather, this is an instruction of the risen Lord, since the title of Lordship itself belongs properly to the risen Jesus, and hence its abiding validity.

that the wife should not separate from her husband (but if she does, let her remain single or else be reconciled to her husband)—and that the husband should not divorce his wife. This only reiterates what we find repeated in Mark 10:11–12; Luke 16:18; and Matt 5:32; 19:9. In the new order of things inaugurated by the coming of Christ into the world, there is simply no place for divorce. Even with the inscrutable "exceptive clause," which Matthew introduces into the command "except on the ground of *porneia*" (Matt 5:32; 19:9), whatever meaning *porneia* may or may not have in this instance, the fact of the interdiction of divorce remains.

78

Because of the multiple attestation of this view in the Gospels, it is all the more important in what follows to keep in mind Paul's awareness that it is the Lord himself who gives this charge.

7:12 To the rest I say, not the Lord,... This leaves no doubt whatever that, in what follows, Paul, fully aware of the Lord's teaching on the matter, goes on to give his own opinion about a specific situation in the Christian community. He offers no excuses. The reason he gives for his opinion is thoroughly consistent with his understanding of Christ's grace and the freedom it confers on the Christian.

that if any brother has a wife who is an unbeliever, and she consents to live with him, he should not divorce her. Because of what future generations of casuists have made of this passage (1 Cor 7:12–15), one needs to keep in mind that Paul has a real marriage in mind. This couple he mentions are truly married, a Christian husband and his unbelieving wife. Had they not been a truly married couple, there could be no talk of divorce.

7:13 If any woman has a husband who is an unbeliever, and he consents to live with her, she should not divorce him. Here again, Paul's evenhandedness in dealing with women and men alike, on equal footing, manifests itself. His statement envisages an alternative situation to that in the previous verse: it is the husband now who happens to be an unbeliever, and his spouse is the Christian. Such marriages at that early state of the church's development must have been very common. The proportion of converts to Christianity so early on will have seen to that. Note, moreover, that it is not statistics, but the free will of the partners that is decisive.

7:14 For the unbelieving husband is consecrated through his wife, and the unbelieving wife is consecrated through her husband. Otherwise, your children would be unclean, but as it is they are holy. Paul does no more here than insist on the premise that holiness is through appurtenance, that it is a consequence of belonging. The unbelieving spouse is "consecrated" through belonging to her or to his believing partner. So, too, are the children of their union. They, too, are holy. How much suffering and heartache would have been spared had Christians been reminded from time to time of this vital fact? If what this verse says of "mixed," that is, believing and unbelieving, partners be true, how much truer would it be of marriages between two Christians!

7:15 But if the unbelieving partner desires to separate, let it be so; in such a case the brother or sister is not bound. For God has called us to peace. One thing must be kept in mind: Paul's only given reason for marriage is the inability of the individual to live without sex. Here we have two people who entered into marriage because they were not made for the celibate life. They chose to enjoy the God-given charism of their sex drive. One of the partners, the unbeliever, is not bound by the Christian ban on divorce and, consequently, is free to go away, for whatever reason, and to marry someone else. This leaves the believing partner, who evidently does not have the charism of sexual abstinence (1 Cor 7:7), to spend his or her days "aflame with passion" (7:9). In such a situation, says Paul, "the brother or sister is not bound." In other words, knowingly, he takes a position in flat contradiction to Jesus' prohibition of divorce.

The reason Paul gives for taking such a position is, as he says, simply that "God has called us to peace." Howsoever you may wish to understand this peace in its present context, whether it be the absence of consuming passion, the cessation of emotional turmoil, or the appeasement of unfulfilled desire, its meaning can, as a famed commentator put it, "relate only to the declaration of freedom." "For freedom Christ has set us free" (Gal 5:1), and nothing and no one must be allowed to encroach upon its exercise by the believer.

A lesson taught by Paul in this passage is all too often over-looked. The New Testament is not a substitute or a replacement for the Old. It is not meant to provide a new set of laws to take the place of the old ones. This is true even of "the very words of Jesus." If we can be sure of one teaching of Jesus, it is the teaching on divorce. Yet, fully cognizant of this, Paul does not hesitate to go against it: "I say, not the Lord" (7:12). Christians are forever asking, "What does the New Testament say?" or "What is the teaching of Jesus?" They are in continuous need of being reminded that the New Testament is simply not that kind of a book, nor is Jesus that kind of a teacher. Neither Jesus nor the New Testament provides answers to queries. They pose questions to whoever has ears to hear, questions they alone and not the institution can answer.

7:16 Wife, how do you know whether you will save your husband? Husband, how do you know whether you will save your wife? Paul reverts to the discussion of the situation before the separation of the partners (7:14). His is an instructive reflection on, as well as a conjecture from, the given premise: the salvation of the unbelieving partner as well as of the children of the marriage is by their belonging to the believing partner. One might well wonder, Why did the fathers of the church overlook this verse when they discussed the fate of dead unbaptized babies? If, moreover, Paul is thinking here of including the unbelieving partner as well as the children of the union under the category of "those sanctified in Christ Jesus, called to be saints" (1 Cor 1:2), then that would only accentuate the tragedy of the departing unbelieving partner.

7:17 Only, let every one lead the life which the Lord has assigned to him, and in which God has called him. This is my rule in all the churches. In an age of ceaseless mobility, where change and alteration are the secret of happiness, when "It's time to change" has become part of today's received wisdom, Paul's words must sound odd indeed. It is harder still for our contemporaries to comprehend that each one's place in life is a grace, is in fact God's calling of each individual. This is not an exhortation to be content with one's lot but an invitation to recognize that whatever is mine, including my present situation and position, is God's gift to me. "What have you that you did not receive?" (1 Cor 4:7). If it is a gift, then it is unearned and unearnable by any means we devise, whether changing our marital status, or our church affiliation, or exchanging one state of life for another. "Man's supreme misfortune is his instability." Our greatest tragedy is that God never finds us where he last left us.

Paul, moreover, reassures the Corinthians that this is what he teaches in all the churches. It is not by way of exception or on some special occasion that he says what he says to them. In fact, it is no more than perfectly good Christian sense that he calls to their attention.

7:18 Was any one at the time of his call already circumcised? Let him not seek to remove the marks of circumcision. Was any one at the time of his call uncircumcised? Let him not seek circumcision. The preceding verse laid the ground for this concrete application. Readers of, for example, Paul's Letter to the Galatians recognize in the question of circumcision more than a physiological phenomenon. If, like Paul, you were circumcised at the time of your conversion to Christianity, then you must "not seek to remove the marks of circumcision." Some Jews at the time sought to do so in order to avoid being recognized, particularly in the baths where much of daily life in the Roman Empire was spent. The surgical procedure involved was so horrendous that Paul's advice seems scarcely necessary.

The reverse situation, however, was a genuine crisis in early Christianity. There were those who, unconvinced of the all-sufficiency of Christ, urged the converts to undergo Mosaic circumcision. Paul's argument against this practice is that "if you receive circumcision, Christ will be of no advantage to you" (Gal 5:2; Rom 2:25). It goes counter to the gift of freedom that the Christian has in Christ Jesus. The fact of the matter is that you who receive circumcision "are bound to keep the whole law" (Gal 5:3); and, consequently, "if you would be justified by the law," then you are "severed from Christ...have fallen away from grace" (Gal 5:4).

7:19 For neither circumcision counts for anything nor uncircumcision, but keeping the commandments of God. The essential to keep

82

in mind is that the issue here is neither circumcision nor uncircumcision, but submission to the will of God. This "keeping the commandments of God" is given its superb formulation in a parallel in Galatians: "For in Christ Jesus neither circumcision nor uncircumcision is of any avail, but faith working [made effective] through love" (5:6). Elsewhere in Galatians, Paul affirms that the only thing that matters is our new status as the "new creation" (6:15). This new creation is made effective in the love it manifests, the love that is God's only command in the new dispensation (Rom 13:8–10).

7:20 *Every one should remain in the state in which he was called.* This verse makes explicit what was stated in 7:17. Change of state is not a way of salvation. Recognition of one's gifts from God is. If the question of circumcision is now passé, that of the married state and celibacy certainly is not. How widespread was, and perhaps still is, the notion of entering religious life as, at least, a surer way to salvation! People who evidently did not possess the charism of celibacy embarked upon a life of the vows to save their souls. The tragedy of so many among them ought to have sufficed as a warning, but it did not. Was there no one to remind so many in the Christian community that the married life could just as well be the life that the Lord assigned to them (1 Cor 7:17)? Insisting that one charism is superior to the other, or that only celibacy is a charism, can lead to a mistaken notion that celibate life is blissful and marriage is not.

7:21 *Were you a slave when called? Never mind. But if you can gain your freedom, avail yourself of the opportunity.* Clearly, this is not an advocacy of slavery. It merely acknowledges a fact and is a ready-to-hand illustration of the principle enunciated in this section: "Every one should remain in the state in which he was called" (7:20). Lest his intention be misunderstood, Paul hastens to add, "But if you can gain your freedom," then by all means do so. Such clarification of meaning was the more necessary in a Christian community like Corinth's, where a sizeable portion of the neo-converts must have been slaves (see 1 Cor 11:21–22). It is no less necessary today, when the concept might be deemed antiquated, but its lived reality is every bit as inexorable.

7:22 *For he who was called in the Lord as a slave is a freedman of the Lord. Likewise he who was free when called is a slave of Christ.* This presupposition underlies all that Paul has to say about freedom and slavery. Freedom is always understood by him as freedom under a master. If the master who owns you is Christ, then you are genuinely free. But if anyone or anything else has possession of you, then you are a slave. Thus, if at the time of your conversion, you are a slave, then you are, paradoxically enough, utterly free once Christ is your master. Similarly, if your earthly master who owns you is himself converted, then, free though he is, he is really "a slave of Christ."

Such a passage in the writings of Paul is not a sociological treatise. Only willfully blinkered ill will could make of him an advocate of slavery. More often than not, such misinterpreters of Paul are themselves slaves in thrall to masters other than Christ, whether the masters be sociological, political, intellectual or, worst of all, spiritual.

7:23 *You were bought with a price; do not become slaves of men.* This reiterates 6:20. It not only reminds the Christians of their infinite value and dignity but also warns them against bartering their exalted status for the bogus accolades of the world. The believers belong to Christ; hence their genuine freedom and great dignity. Should they yield to the lure of anyone or anything else, however highly esteemed or holy or seemingly desirable, then their true freedom is forfeit, and their newfound status, whether they know it or not, is slavery.

Christians can never be sufficiently reminded that the price paid for their priceless liberty and for the exalted position that is theirs is nothing less than the precious blood of Christ (1 Pet 1:19). That they are so incredibly ready to barter away this privilege for the counterfeit baubles of wealth, power, and prestige that the world offers them ought to be cause for wonder and astonishment. Yet it is not!

7:24 So, brethren, in whatever state each was called, there let him remain with God. The conclusion is simply the reaffirmation of the principle enunciated in 7:17: "Only, let every one lead the life which the Lord has assigned to him, and in which God has called him. This is my rule in all the churches." Therein lies our only true peace, as in Dante's *E'n la sua volontade è nostra pace* ("In his will is our peace").

7:25 Now concerning the unmarried [NRSV: virgins], I have no command of the Lord, but I give my opinion as one who by the Lord's mercy is trustworthy. Paul's language is a salutary reminder that church authorities can sometimes achieve more cooperation and obedience by the use of a phrase like "I have no command..."

Having dealt first with the unmarried and the widows (7:10–11, 12–16), Paul turns his attention to "the virgins," as the NRSV renders the Greek literally. The Greek term, here and elsewhere (7:28, 34, 36, 37, 38), is *parthenos* and signifies a young nubile maiden, that is, a girl of marriage age but not married. Paul knows of no express command of the Lord in their regard and is not afraid to say so. But, of course, that is not what the New Testament is all about. It is not an answer book to every question that the daily life of the faith tosses up. Paul does only what all ministers of the Word are expected to do: give his own opinion "as one who by the Lord's mercy is trustworthy."

Such trustworthiness is, to be sure, by the grace of the Lord, but, like all grace, it brings with it the obligation of responsible hard work. The minister of the Word is never exempt from doing her or his homework (see, for example, Galatians 1:17; 2:1: those fourteen long years after Paul's conversion were, surely, not spent in tourism). Not only is Paul's approach to the question of virgins exemplary, but his point-by-point consideration of its different aspects is instructive. There is an impartiality in theologizing that is as beautiful to comprehend as it is to contemplate.

7:26 I think that in view of the present distress it is well for a person to remain as he is. Paul's ever-present conviction of the imminence of the end provides another argument in favor of maintaining one's status, to "remain as he is." Even if the argument itself is baseless, even if, as it turned out, the catastrophe of the end proved not to be near, Paul's opinion still stands. For, in the Christian scheme of things, where you are here and now is where God finds you. Your position, your occupation, your marital status, are all God's gift to you, God's will for you, "the life which the Lord has assigned" you (7:17).

7:27 Are you bound to a wife? Do not seek to be free. Are you free from a wife? Do not seek marriage. Paul returns to the principal question at hand: marriage and celibacy. What he says here is not said absolutely; marriage is not being abolished (see 7:2, 28, 36). Nor is he proposing a lofty ascetical ideal. Saint Augustine says in the *City of God*, "Just because something is difficult does not make it good; anymore than its being stupid make it healthy." What Paul does say here is said in the eschatological context of the impending end. If the parousia, the second coming, is just around the corner, then what Paul says here would make perfectly good sense. The reasons he provides in the next few verses for his opinion notwithstanding, he still insists that, if you cannot live without it, then go ahead and get married (7:28). It is no sin.

Much too important a lesson is offered us in these verses (7:25–35) to go unnoticed. Paul's expectations of the end were mistaken, and twenty-one centuries of elapsed time is there to prove it. Nevertheless, Christian history is full of this error of judgment, recurring every generation, including our own. Paul's excuse might well be that he had "no command of the Lord" on this matter (7:25). But the generations that followed him could not reasonably claim such an excuse. There, for all to see in the Gospel of Matthew, Jesus himself declares, "But of that day and hour no one knows, not even the angels of heaven, nor the Son, but the Father only" (Matt 24:36; Mark 13:32). If Paul himself happened not to be acquainted with this teaching of the Master in the tradition, then subsequent generations, which knew Matthew's Gospel like no other, could not plead similar ignorance.

7:28 But if you marry, you do not sin, and if a girl [NRSV: a virgin] marries she does not sin. How admirably Paul keeps in mind that he is not proclaiming a "command of the Lord" (1 Cor 7:25) but only giving expression to his own opinion. He wants no mistake whatever on that score: marriage is not a sin, not even on the eve of the "great day of the Lord" (Zeph 1:14).

Yet those who marry will have worldly troubles, and I would spare you that. It seems reasonable to assume that those who marry "in view of the impending crisis" (1 Cor 7:26) will have far greater troubles in their daily lives than those who don't marry, although even this view is merely speculative. Laudable though Paul's desire to spare married people the trouble is, that day itself is still an unknown, and everything about it is still a conjecture. If ever in doubt, refer to Jesus's words in Matthew 24:36.

7:29–31 I mean, brethren, the appointed time has grown very short;... One has to wonder just how Paul came by this conviction. Doubtless, there have been biblical interpreters who analyze the sources of Paul's beliefs about the proximity of the end. But, because that conviction itself was to prove baseless, could its sources have been any less so? Had Paul been alive today, two millennia after the fact, what reason, one wonders, would he have invented for his opinion?

from now on, let those who have wives live as though they had none, and those who mourn as though they were not mourning, and those who rejoice as though they were not rejoicing, and those who buy as though they had no goods, and those who deal with the world as though they had no dealings with it. All too often, a wrong premise can yield perfectly valid conclusions. The series gives us an unexceptionable description of the life of the Christian in the world "between the times," between the Creed's "He ascended into heaven" and "He will come again to judge the living and the dead."

The hyperbole almost inherent in this genre of writing apart, what Paul says is simply that those who live in the world in these eschatological times—and all genuinely Christian times are eschatological—should jealously guard their freedom by refusing to be enslaved by anyone or anything (1 Cor 7:22–23): neither by their spouses, nor by their travails and suffering, nor by their joys, nor by their possessions or their occupation. This advice is valid whether the Lord will come tomorrow or several eons hence.

For the form of this world is passing away. The ultimate reason why subjection to any of the above creaturely entities is in fact a thralldom is that they are creatures and are, therefore, mutable, perishable, and ultimately mortal. Paul urges the Christian to shun slavery to any created thing whatsoever simply because we have, and can have, no master but Jesus Christ. Belonging exclusively to him, being "freedmen of the Lord," is our only true liberty (1 Cor 7:22).

7:32 I want you to be free from anxieties. The unmarried man is anxious about the affairs of the Lord, how to please the Lord;... The context is still eschatological. But, whether it is or not, the absence of anxiety is always an indispensable condition for the dedicated service of the Lord. Paul's expressed wish here and in Philippians 4:6, "Have no anxiety about anything," are the requisites for that "peace of God, which passes all understanding" (Phil 4:7) to dwell in our hearts. This is why the embolism of the Our Father in the liturgy prays that we be delivered "from all anxiety" and not, as the self-appointed pseudo-psychologists of the liturgy pretend, "from all *unnecessary* anxiety." One is often tempted to cry out, "That's not the same anxiety!"

The celibate can well devote his or her life to the service of the Lord and not necessarily behind monastery walls. Anyone who has the experience knows how remarkably even a little anxiety (*merimna*) can distract the believer, married or single, not just in prayer but in the ordinary tasks of serving the other. If you add to this Paul's conviction of the impending end, and remember the small size of the nascent Christian community in Corinth, you can readily comprehend his desire and his prayer that the believers be "free from anxiety."

7:33–34 but the married man is anxious about worldly affairs [NRSV: the affairs of the world], how to please his wife, and his interests are divided. This is by no means a demotion of the married state but the statement of an everyday empirical fact. The interests of such a person are, inevitably, divided. Perhaps the best way to grasp the true meaning of the statement is to compare it with what Paul says elsewhere about his own life in the ministry: "And, apart from other things, there is the daily pressure upon me of my anxiety for all the churches" (2 Cor 11:28). Paul's "anxiety for all the churches" is an integral part of his anxiety "about the affairs of the Lord" (1 Cor 7:32), which is quite distinct from the married man's anxiety "about the affairs of the world."

And the unmarried woman or girl [NRSV: virgin] is anxious about the affairs of the Lord, how to be holy in body and spirit;... The life of holiness has its exigencies. Continual vigilance is its price. Holiness of life is for all ages and all states of life. It involves the totality of the person, which is what Paul means by "body and spirit" in this context. This is not the Platonic dichotomy with which we are all familiar, but a biblical expression to encompass the whole person, as in "you shall love the LORD your God with all your heart, and with all your soul, and with all your might" (Deut 6:5, and see Mark 12:30).

but the married woman is anxious about worldly affairs, how to please her husband. The RSV's "worldly affairs" gives the impression of a pejorative sense. The Greek, however, as the NRSV correctly translates, has "the affairs of the world." In other words, the statement merely repeats, albeit in a different context, "Therefore a man leaves his father and his mother and cleaves to his wife"

(Gen 2:24; Mark 10:7; Matt 19:5). Again, this merely states a laudable fact and not a negative judgment. What ingenious misinterpretations this passage (1 Cor 7:32–34) has been subjected to in the course of history would constitute a whole encyclopedia of mental teratologies.

7:35 I say this for your own benefit, not to lay any restraint upon you, but to promote good order and to secure your undivided devotion to the Lord. Here's another example of Paul's approach to the community "with love in a spirit of gentleness" (1 Cor 4:21). The reminder that he is not promulgating a law or adding a new "restraint" on the Corinthians is all the more necessary because of their—and our—inveterate tendency to regard loving advice as minatory judgment. What Paul says here he says "for their benefit." His whole purpose in saying it is not their subjugation to his authority but the desire to secure their undivided service and devotion to the Lord, not, as happens so frequently and regularly, to someone in authority, or to some institution, or some ideology.

7:36 If any one thinks that he is not behaving properly toward his betrothed [NRSV: virgin], if his passions are strong, and it has to be, let him do as he wishes: let them marry—it is no sin. Although the description of the relationship strikes many as archaic, a moment's reflection will reveal just how accurate it is. All love seeks union. If the impulse becomes, as in the present case, irresistibly intense, then the person should go ahead and marry his beloved, even if the second coming were just around the corner, "in view of the impending distress" (7:25). Marriage is not a sin. It never is (7:28, 36). What is a sin is to have sex outside marriage. You might choose to deny this point of view, argue against it, or dismiss it as irrelevant altogether, but there is no gainsaying the fact that it is Paul's firm point of view. Anyone who grants Paul's presuppositions in these matters ("Do you not know that your bodies are members of Christ?…Do you not know that your body is a temple of the Holy Spirit within you.…You were bought with a price"; 1 Cor 6:15, 19–20) cannot do otherwise, cannot pick and choose among the statements in this chapter.

7:37 *But whoever is firmly established in his heart, being under no necessity but having his desire under control, and has determined this in his heart, to keep her as his betrothed [NRSV: virgin], he will do well.* This is still "in view of the impending distress," in the firm conviction that the second coming, the parousia, is imminent. Paul is consistent in his views on this matter. Moreover, what he says here in view of the approaching end would have made no sense at all had he expected the days ahead to stretch into the indefinite future. His concluding instruction on marriage, sex, and celibacy is not meant to annul the divine command to "Be fruitful and multiply, and fill the earth" (Gen 1:28).

Several provisos are to be taken into account in heeding Paul's advice. First of all, in keeping with the way he always deals with the community entrusted to his care, he insists that in this particular circumstance the individual is "under no necessity." Paul is not laying down a law; he is simply counseling, giving advice. Second, he insists on the autonomy and intelligence of the individual involved, who must judge for himself whether he can keep his sex urge under control even as he faces an indefinite period of time of living with his beloved. This self-control is not an asceticism nor a test of endurance. Strange though it may sound to some contemporary ears, the resolve to live in this way with his beloved might well be the supreme token of the genuinity of his love for her.

Finally, Paul simply says such a person "will do well." He applauds a possible choice between two alternatives without passing condemnatory judgment on either, as he makes clear in the following:

7:38 *So that he who marries his betrothed does well; and he who refrains from marriage will do better.* The "he does well" should be taken strictly indeed. There is no sin whatever involved in the person's choice to marry (7:28, 36). Apart the sobriety of his opinion in this matter, Paul knows this is not a concession to human weakness but the recognition of a God-given gift. Paul knows, as we sometimes choose not to know, that both the strong passions and the self-control to govern them are gifts of God and not instruments of Satan.

That he "who refrains from marriage" does better expresses no more than the understandable prejudice of a man who wishes that "all were as I myself am" (7:7). Never does he say that the alternative to this state, which happens to be his, is bad or a sin. A small but important grammatical point is to be kept in mind: the *and* in this verse is not, as so very many have misread it, adversative but conjunctive. In other words, the *and* does not contrast two states but merely juxtaposes them.

7:39 *A wife is bound to her husband as long as he lives. If the husband dies, she is free to be married to whom she wishes, only in the Lord.* Paul now takes up the case of widows in the community where, in all likelihood, they were numerous. Here, too, one must keep in mind that this widow got married in the first place because she chose not to embrace a life of celibacy. It is very likely she still does not choose to forego the married life. She is "free," or as Romans puts it, "If her husband dies she is discharged from the law concerning the husband" (Rom 7:2), that is, she is free to remarry. The only condition—if it might be called that—is that she marry "in the Lord," a fellow Christian. Nevertheless, one might also read the "in the Lord" as applicable rather to her freedom of choice to remarry. Perhaps such a reading is favored also by Romans 7:2.

7:40 *But in my judgment she is happier if she remains as she is. And I think that I have the Spirit of God.* Comprehensible though his properly qualified personal opinion is, "in my judgment," it says no more than he "who refrains from marriage will do better" in 7:38. Paul is not legislating, only offering personal opinion, however valuable and worthy of respect. Perhaps Saint Augustine, and who better, said it best when in the *Confessions* he prays, "You, O

Lord, forbade fornication, permitted marriage, and offered me something better."

"And I think I have the Spirit of God" is a commonplace in religious literature (Deut 4:2; Ezra 6:11; Jer 11:3; Rev 22:19), a concluding rhetorical *boutade*, if you will. Yet, account must be taken of the "I think" in the sentence. Such a remark could equally have been made by the Christian widow, whether she chose to remarry or to remain as she is. She was in a better position to judge her happiness in one state or the other than Paul or anyone else.

Chapter 8

FIRST CORINTHIANS 8

8:1 Now concerning food offered to idols: we know that "all of us possess knowledge." The opening phrase, "Now concerning," signals another question put to Paul in the letter from Corinth (7:1, 25; 8:4; 12:1; 16:1, 12). Perhaps no other topic in the epistle is farther removed from our present situation. Nevertheless, for sheer relevance, it is hard to find a topic that surpasses the content of this chapter. Food offered to idols is well-nigh meaningless to most Christians today. But the problems it gave rise to in Corinth are every bit as weighty, or as pertinent to Christian conduct today, as any raised in the epistle.

The slogan-loving Corinthians have another compendious *bon mot* to take care of the problem. "All of us possess knowledge." We are all intelligent enough to know that idols do not exist. So, to speak of food offered to idols cannot possibly be a problem for the Christian believer. Or, at least, so did those who boasted of their knowledge think.

"Knowledge" puffs up, but love builds up. As is his wont, Paul does not deny the truth of the Corinthians' slogan but distinguishes between the effect of knowledge and that of love. The reason the RSV puts the word "knowledge" in quotation marks, as the NRSV does not, is most likely to call attention to the technical use of the term. "Knowledge," in fact, translates *gnosis*, which was not just a phenomenon of the human spirit but a system of thought that might well have been the first Christian heresy. For our present purpose, it is enough to keep in mind the link of this knowledge to the wisdom that so bewitched the Corinthians (1 Cor 1:18–25;

2:1–5, 6–15). The quest for knowledge, like that for wisdom, can beget pride, and "puff up."

The antidote to the pride, which regards the self, is love, which looks to the interests of the other, that is, "builds up." Building up is one of the essential Pauline concepts in this epistle, as we shall have occasion to see (8:10; 10:23; 14:3, 4, 5, 17, 26). What is important at this juncture is to keep in mind both the basic truth of the slogan that all of us possess knowledge, and the qualification that must be borne in mind in its practical application.

8:2 If any one imagines that he knows something, he does not yet know as he ought to know. Those who say "All of us possess knowledge" need to be reminded that knowledge, this side of the great chasm between time and eternity, is never perfect or, put more pejoratively, is always defective. It is never easy to convince those who claim to possess knowledge that theirs is imperfect, defective. Socrates had the impossible task of persuading his countrymen that true wisdom consists in recognizing that you know nothing. His task in our times cannot even bear contemplating, especially because of our tendency to confound information with knowledge and, worse still, to confuse knowledge with wisdom. A character in one of Simone de Beauvoir's novels asks, When did simple folk lose the sense of "truly human values"? and is told, "The day knowledge was preferred to wisdom."

8:3 But if one loves God, one is known by him. The contrast with the imperfection of knowledge is love, the love of God, which admits of no gradation. One either loves God and lives, which is what "is known by him" means, or does not. There can be no middle ground, no third option. This is why Exodus says the Lord "is a jealous God" (Exod 34:14; 20:5; Deut 5:9). This love of God constitutes the only true wisdom. All else is folly (1 Cor 1:21, 25).

8:4 Hence, as to the eating of food offered to idols, we know that "an idol has no real existence," and that "there is no God but one." Like many an ancient city's, Corinth's temples of the gods were kept busy daily with the sacrifice of animals, usually ungulates, sheep, heifers, calves, and the like. The priests, who assisted at the daily sacrifices, cut a small choice morsel of the animal and tossed it into the fire to propitiate the deity. The rest of the carcass was sold to the butchers, eateries, and marketplaces of the city. With the daily abundance of such sacrifices, there was no meat to be had that did not come from the pagan sacrifices in the temples. Ultimately, all food served in Corinth, at home or in the market, was "food offered to idols."

Now, the Christians of Corinth "knew" that no idol had any real existence. They also believed firmly, as the first article of their creed, that "there is no God but one." Nothing could be more logically consistent than these two propositions, which may or may not have been part of the repertoire of the Corinthians' slogans. The quotation marks supplied by both the RSV and the NRSV are exegetical, the translators' interpretation. The Greek text, of course, had no such punctuation marks. The phrases could just as well have been phrases from the confession of faith recited by the Corinthians.

8:5 *For although there may be so-called gods in heaven or on earth—as indeed there are many "gods" and many "lords"...* The recrudescence of quotation marks in this section was, doubtless, deemed necessary to ward off misunderstanding. Whose misunderstanding, however, is hard to determine. The Gentile converts had no need to be told that the background whence they emerged was polytheistic, abounding in deities, temples, and cults. The converts from Judaism, on the other hand, needed no reminder of the abominations of the nations. Their fierce monotheism shone in stark contrast in a world full of gods, goddesses, and deities.

8:6 *yet for us there is one God, the Father, from whom are all things and for whom we exist,...* The credal affirmation is, by contrast, perfectly apropos. It reminds the believers, who in every age stand in need of being reminded that the only God they worship is the source of everything, including the "food offered to idols," and is also the end toward that all creation tends. The poet put it best:

Thee, God, I come from, to thee go,
All day long I like fountain flow...

This God is now revealed as Father: the Father of Jesus Christ and our Father. So, in a still more profound sense, the God we worship is the Father who begot us and to whom we wend our way home.

and one Lord, Jesus Christ, through whom are all things and through whom we exist. The continuation of the credal confession makes clear why, in the previous verse (8:5), Paul mentioned both "many gods" and many "lords." The Christian confession of faith acknowledges one only God, the Father, and one only Lord, Jesus Christ his Son. It is through this Son that all things came to be, just as the Father is he "from whom are all things." It is also through the Son that "we exist," just as it is for the Father that "we exist." This is one of the rich sources out of which the doctrine of the Trinity will eventually draw its constitutive elements.

How appropriate it is to be reminded, precisely at this juncture, of what must be continually before our eyes, particularly when we risk getting bewildered in some engrossing problem like "food offered to idols." It has been so long since these fundamental truths of the faith made the passage from formulae to life that we have become immune to their power. Consequently, we have become inextricably embroiled in problems of our own making and distracted from the true mainsprings of our lives. Those who pretend this is incomprehensible are invited to draw up their elenchus of the current major concerns of the church and set them against the words in 1 Corinthians 8:6. Better still, ask any man in the street what the Catholic Church teaches.

8:7 However, not all possess this knowledge. The understanding of these words has to be in two tiers. Paul merely reminds the

Corinthians that, all their claims to the contrary notwithstanding, not all of them possess knowledge (8:1). The Christian community is not an academy. Indeed, one might readily suspect the reason behind our own current preoccupation with the problems that occupy the church is simply that everyone and everybody claims to "possess knowledge." In today's language, "We are all theologians!" At the same time, the neglect of the essentials of the faith, which is the casualty both of today's political correctness and bogus pretentiousness, is only a threadbare excuse for the prevalent theological ignorance. When, occasionally, such ignorance is exposed, the stock evasion is "After all, I am not a theologian!" or "I leave these to the experts!" as though divine revelation was there only to provide job security for university professors.

The second tier of understanding "not all possess this knowledge" is the easily discernible divide in the Christian community between those who are strong and those who are weak (Rom 15:1). The former know what they believe and have the courage to act upon it. They possess both conviction and resolve. The weak, on the other hand, think they know what they believe, but their grasp of it is shaky at best and largely dependent on others for its momentary flashes of unwarranted boldness. The rest of the verse furnishes an admirable illustration of their case.

But some, through being hitherto accustomed to idols, eat food as really offered to an idol; and their conscience, being weak, is defiled. The habits and convictions of a lifetime die hard. This Gentile convert lived his religion fervently and worshiped his gods with piety. The new religion assured him there are no gods at all, but only one unique God, the Father, and one Lord, his Son, Jesus Christ. The convert affirms this no less fervently and sincerely. But, from time to time, a severe test of his faith comes along, as in the case of "food offered to idols." Deep down in his heart he cannot shake his old convictions. If he believes the gods somehow still exist, eating meat offered to them would still be for him a sin. For whatever reason, either to avoid seeming singular, or fearing

98

to betray his misgivings, or in a vain effort to prove his imagined strength, this weak person goes ahead and eats the food offered him and thereby "defiles" his conscience.

Conscience is a favorite in our current vocabulary. But it is good to keep in mind that the Greek word as employed in the New Testament, and translated here as "conscience," does not mean what we usually understand by the term. In fact, it is a retrospective judgment on an act that has already taken place (for example, Rom 2:15; 2 Cor 1:12). It is not, as we use the term today, an antecedent, prospective judgment about what I am about to do or to refrain from doing. It is not formed; it informs.

8:8 *Food will not commend us to God. We are no worse off if we do not eat, and no better off if we do.* Paul very adroitly removes the argument from where it does not belong. All such acts as eating and drinking, sleeping and waking, and what have you are in and of themselves neutral acts. For centuries, these and similar examples of human activity have been the stock in trade of moralists in Christianity. In themselves the acts neither please nor displease the Almighty. You are no better off if you do them and no worse off if you don't. This seems like an otiose reminder of the obvious. Yet, if it was necessary to remind the Corinthians of it, how much more necessary is it to remember it today?

8:9 *Only take care lest this liberty of yours somehow become a stumbling block to the weak.* The possession of knowledge allows you the exercise of your freedom, the "All things are lawful for me" (6:12; 10:23), but it ought also to show you its limits. The "other" always defines the limits of that freedom, not by restricting it, nor by curtailing its exercise, but by indicating where it ceases to be freedom and becomes something else altogether. This is why Saint Augustine says, "You want to know what kind of love is yours? Look where it leads." If it transgresses its limits by disregarding the good of the other, then it is no longer freedom but license. It is no longer love. Therefore, while not denying that "all

99

things are lawful," Paul insists that not "all things are helpful," "not all things build up" (6:12; 10:23).

The Christian, therefore, must ever be on the alert lest the exercise of her or his liberty become the cause of harm to the neighbor. Our freedom is not only a freedom *from*, but also and especially a freedom *for*: "For freedom Christ has set us free" (Gal 5:1). As we shall have occasion to see, it is ultimately a freedom to love, and whatever offends against love, whatever proves a "stumbling block to the weak," is a curtailment of freedom.

8:10 For if any one sees you, a man of knowledge, at table in an idol's temple, might he not be encouraged, if his conscience is weak, to eat food offered to idols? This is a variant of the "Everybody is doing it" syndrome of our day. You need not have read Darwin to be an evolutionist. All you need is to be aware of how much of the ape is in all of us. It is arguable that more people have fallen by imitation than by intention. To the eye of "the weak" in the Christian community, the strong is always the "man of knowledge." Down the centuries, those who minister to the Christian community, in whatever capacity, have always been put, rightly or wrongly, in this latter category.

Deep down in his heart, the weak believes, however vaguely, that idols exist. Because he believes they do, even if in fact they have no existence whatsoever, he sins if he eats meat offered to them. What gives him the courage he needs is the example of the strong who thinks nothing of sitting at table "in an idol's temple." It is scarcely reductionist to affirm that the freedom of the strong in this instance is the cause of the sin of the weak. It takes a giant's strength of will to adhere to one's unpopular convictions in disregard of what the mighty and those held in high esteem do. How many mortals possess such strength of will?

To be sure, meat offered to idols is very far from our present concerns. But the situation described in Corinth and the warning issued to the Corinthians, "Only take care lest this liberty of yours somehow become a stumbling block" (8:9), are every bit as applicable to us today. One need only consider the case of adolescents in our society and the periodic pandemics of evil they fall victim to. All the instruction and exhortation of family and church and school cannot outweigh the might of peer example, the thralldom of counterfeit heroes.

8:11 And so by your knowledge this weak man is destroyed, the brother for whom Christ died. Strong but accurate language is employed to formulate the only genuinely valid moral principle of action in Christian life. If, as was mentioned earlier (see in 8:8), human acts are, in and of themselves, neutral, what confers on them their moral ponderousness is the "other." To destroy this other in the exercise of my God-given freedom is my sin of sins. Not only is the other a temple of the Holy Spirit (6:19) but is in fact the one for whom Christ died. Each one of them has been bought with a price (6:20), the precious blood of Christ (1 Pet 1:19). Therein lies, to take but one palmary instance, the true evil of sin in, for example, sexual matters. All the other reasons proffered in moral instructions dwindle into insignificance by comparison. Would that "the brother for whom Christ died" become a major premise in moral theology. It would surely trump other designations of "the other."

8:12 Thus, sinning against your brethren and wounding their conscience when it is weak, you sin against Christ. Paul carries the argument one step further, to its logical conclusion: to destroy "the brother for whom Christ died" is in fact to "sin against Christ." This should be a familiar truth from the New Testament: "As you did it to one of these least of these my brethren you did it to me" (Matt 25:40, 45; John 15:18). To inflict such a wound on the conscience of the weak sister or brother in the exercise of my liberty is a sin, in the strict acceptation of the term. It is an offense against Christ, as Paul will succinctly put it in Romans: "If your brother is being injured by what you eat, you are no longer walking in love. Do not let what you eat cause the ruin of one for whom Christ died" (Rom 14:15).

8:13 Therefore, if food is a cause of my brother's falling [Greek: if food scandalizes my brother], I will never eat meat, lest I cause my brother to fall. The temptation to dismiss this concluding statement as hyperbole robs it of its true import. It stresses what cannot be sufficiently stressed: the infinite worth of the brother, and the awful responsibility of each believer. You cannot require people to do such a thing; you cannot even counsel them to do it. What Paul says here is the spontaneous, untrammeled exercise of his Christian freedom. This lies on the other far side of all moral injunctions, well beyond the demands of the Ten Commandments.

Chapter 9

FIRST CORINTHIANS 9

9:1 Am I not free? Am I not an apostle? Have I not seen Jesus our Lord? Are not you my workmanship in the Lord? The abrupt chain of questions leaves the reader of two minds: either Paul is readying for a change of subject, or he is about to illustrate his own use of the freedom that is his in Christ Jesus. Although all the questions appear to be rhetorical, with Paul expecting a positive answer, one of them, shuffled into the middle, cannot be given such an unqualified response. Paul is undoubtedly free; he is certainly an apostle (1 Cor 1:1; 2 Cor 1:1; Gal 1:1; Rom 1:1); and the Corinthians are evidently his "workmanship." But, as to his having "seen Jesus our Lord," we do believe what he says, although we have to confess our ignorance of its precise meaning. You have to ask what "see" means here: Is it the same as when the disciples saw him in the resurrection appearances (1 Cor 15:5)? Or is it as several great mystics claim to have seen the Lord? Or is it Paul's own interpretation of his road to Damascus experience (Gal 1:16, 12; 2 Cor 12:1, 7)? In a case like this, our ignorance demands a prudent silence. Those who rush to offer an answer are most to be suspected. Ignorance is all too often rashly glib.

9:2 If to others I am not an apostle, at least I am to you; for you are the seal of my apostleship in the Lord. It is comforting, perhaps even endearing, to recognize so deeply a human trait in someone like Paul. He cannot bring himself to forget the attack on his status as an apostle. Evidence of this can be found in the opening of several of his epistles (Romans, 1 and 2 Corinthians, Galatians), and particularly in the bitter polemic of Second Corinthians (11:5, 13;

12:11, 12). The genuineness and the legitimacy of his apostleship do matter. In his status as one sent, which is what *apostle* means, lies his authority and authorization to proclaim the gospel.

To the Corinthians at least, the fact that Paul preached the gospel to them ought to put the question of his apostleship beyond contention. The community of believers in Corinth is, as it were, the sign manual of Paul's apostleship, the seal of its authenticity in the Lord.

9:3 *This is my defense to those who would examine me.* The defense Paul mounts is, in all likelihood, against the very Corinthians who led the mob in praise and adulation when first they met him. It is astonishing what small, seemingly insignificant matters can ignite opposition and rouse hatred of someone who, but a short while ago, was cherished and esteemed. Nothing delights the mob more than the chance to march in the funeral cortege of whatever seemed to them immortal. Corinth was no different from any modern diocese, any more than it was different from that crowd that one day shouted alleluias and the next cried, "Crucify him!"

9:4 *Do we not have the right to our food and drink?* What is the right of every hardworking woman or man suddenly becomes a contentious issue in those who preach the gospel. The wild frenetic swings of opinion on such matters seem incomprehensible. One day, nothing is too good for those who minister to the people; the next day, even ordinary "food and drink" is begrudged them. This is why the saintly founders of orders in the history of the church wished to embrace poverty and to adopt an austere manner of life. Of course, not all their followers, perhaps not even the majority, lived the ideal. But, when the time came, all were indiscriminately traduced as gluttons and wine-bibbers.

9:5 *Do we not have the right to be accompanied by a wife [NRSV: a believing wife; Greek: a sister as wife], as the other apostles and the brothers of the Lord and Cephas?* However one may wish to render the Greek text, which in fact says "sister wife," the essential to keep in mind is the right of the apostle to be accompanied by a female companion. This verse is surely relevant to reflection about married clergy. One assumes that it influenced the views of the Orthodox churches, and it should be part of any debate about married clergy.

Those enumerated by Paul, "the other apostles and the brothers of the Lord and Cephas," were evidently married men, not widowers or siblings. There is clear New Testament evidence for at least one of them: Cephas, or Simon, or Peter (Mark 1:30; Matt 8:14; Luke 4:38). We have been accustomed to add tacitly, whenever mention is made of Peter's wife, that she, of course, had passed away in the meantime. No one seemed disposed to ask, How do we know this? What evidence have we for it? The ecclesiastical historian Eusebius (260–340) cites Saint Clement of Alexandria (end of the second century) without any fanfare or explanation:

> Clement…with respect to those who reject marriage gives a list of the Apostles who were known to have been married, saying: "Or will they disapprove even the Apostles? For Peter and Philip begot children, and Philip, too, gave his daughters to husbands, and Paul [Phil 4:3; 1 Cor 9:5, 13] does not hesitate in an Epistle to address his wife, whom he did not take about with him that he might facilitate the ministry."

9:6 Or is it only Barnabas and I who have no right to refrain from working for a living? For carping criticism, either end of a cudgel will do. Had Paul and Barnabas entered into collective bargaining with their congregations, they would have been readily labeled greedy exploiters, dishonest, luxury seekers, and so on. But now the situation is the reverse: Paul and Barnabas choose to serve the community gratis, and yet their right to do so is challenged. They could well have retorted with the householder in the parable, "Am I not allowed to do what I choose with what belongs to me? Or do you begrudge my generosity?" (Matt 20:15).

9:7 Who serves as a soldier at his own expense? Who plants a vineyard without eating any of its fruit? Who tends a flock without getting some of the milk? In every walk of life "the laborer deserves his wages" (1 Tim 5:18). By means of these rhetorical questions, Paul builds up his case step by step. He wants to establish beyond any doubt that he and Barnabas possess the right to be compensated for their labors. His first argument is from ordinary common sense, which, nevertheless, in Corinth as in our own time seems not to be so common. Hence, the need to state it.

9:8–9 Do I say this on human authority? Does not the law say the same? For it is written in the law of Moses, "You shall not muzzle an ox when it is treading out the grain." Is it for oxen that God is concerned? Paul elevates the argument from human common sense to divine law (Deut 25:4). In typically biblical idiom, the argument sets down the law that human labor merits compensation. Lest his hearers evade the implication of the Mosaic legislation, Paul makes clear that the law has in its purview human beings, not animal husbandry. Should this seem like belaboring the obvious, we can reflect how in our own times it is not infrequently observed that human beings are "muzzled" while quadrupeds are pampered.

9:10 Does he not speak entirely for our sake? It was written for our sake, because the plowman should plow in hope and the thresher thresh in hope of a share in the crop. Paul's insistence on the obvious should alert us to the importance he attaches to this point. If he chooses to forego his wages, it is to prove, paradoxically enough, that he has an undeniable right to them. You can only give up what you have a right to in the first place. The hope of reward is a mighty incentive in all human endeavor, and Paul is eager to have the Corinthians keep this in mind.

In the argument proposed here, we are reminded that the words of the law are "entirely for our sake," "written for our sake." Once again, a self-evident truth has been stood on its head. The lives of so many Christians are lived as if entirely for the sake of the law. Desire to conform with its requirements, and care to avoid violating its decrees, accompanies many a Christian life from start to finish. This might at first blush seem admirable, but its inevitable concomitant is the loss of our freedom in Christ. Should one be tempted to regard this paragraph as no more than an arbitrary digression, keep in mind that Paul's whole argument is precisely about the liberty he possesses and the rights he enjoys.

9:11 If we have sown spiritual good among you, is it too much if we reap your material benefits? To be sure, spiritual goods are, unlike material benefits, imponderables. Yet, for all that, they do consume time and require energy for their exercise. Consequently, they do merit material recompense, however incommensurable it ultimately proves to be.

The problem of recompense for so-called spiritual goods has not left us. In Paul's time, it was the stipends expected by itinerant philosophers and the "superlative apostles" in Corinth (2 Cor 11:5; 12:11). At the time of the Crusades and the Reformation, it was indulgences. In our times, it is those who "peddle" (2 Cor 2:17) spiritual wares by the hour, what the French refer to in another context as *services tarifés*. The reason behind the success of such endeavors in any age is the tacit conviction that "money can buy everything," even eternal salvation.

9:12 If others share this rightful claim upon you, do not we still more? The protracted argument is brought to a conclusion with a rhetorical device called *a minore ad majus* ("from lesser to greater"). If others have claims on the Corinthians, how much more he who is their apostle, whose workmanship they are (1 Cor 9:1–2)?

Nevertheless, we have not made use of this right, but we endure anything rather than put an obstacle in the way of the gospel of Christ. A medieval saying insists that you cannot give what you haven't got. Paul expended many words to establish decisively that he did indeed have such a right before he reminds the Corinthians that he freely, of his own will, gave it up, chose not to make use of it. He goes on to explain the motive behind his decision: he simply did

107

not want "to put an obstacle in the way of the gospel of Christ." Money and its homologues have ever been such obstacles.

For all the genuine generosity that often inspires it, and despite all the protestations to the contrary, material recompense for the ministry can, and often does, hamper its very object, the proclamation of the gospel. On the part of the ministers, acquisitiveness is comprehensible enough. The vow of poverty that many of them take is scarcely a remedy. It frequently aggravates the symptoms. Many of those who vowed poverty succeeded in discovering hitherto unsuspected meanings in Paul's boast of "having nothing and yet possessing all things" (2 Cor 6:10).

The ready generosity of the poor and rich alike in the church can be a truly edifying spectacle; but at the same time it can be something else altogether. Crudely put, buying one's way into heaven is not the joke it seems. The homilies of someone like Saint John Chrysostom are only one example of the lucidity about the donors and benefactors of the church as well as their motives. Great benefactions to monasteries and churches were, more often than not, accompanied by the neglect of the poor and of one's neighbor. Of course, the often questionable means of acquiring the wealth that made the benefactions possible made them suspect. On this latter theme, the prophets of old pronounced some memorable indictments:

> "What do you mean by crushing my people, by grinding the face of the poor?" says the Lord GOD of hosts. (Isa 3:15)

> Woe to those who decree iniquitous decrees, and the writers who keep writing oppression, to turn aside the needy from justice and to rob the poor of my people of their right, that widows may be their spoil, and that they may make the fatherless their prey! (Isa 10:12)

Behold, this was the guilt of your sister Sodom: she and her daughters had pride, surfeit of food, and prosperous ease, but did not aid the poor and needy. (Ezek 16:49)

...they that trample the head of the poor into the dust of the earth, and turn aside the way of the afflicted... (Amos 2:7)

The pastoral epistles, too, summed up the matter in "love of money is the root of all evil" (1 Tim 6:10) and stipulated specifically that "a bishop must be...no lover of money" (3:3). For the Old Testament denunciations as for the neglect of the New Testament prescriptions, the daily newspapers provide frequent lamentable examples.

9:13 *Do you not know that those who are employed in the temple service get their food from the temple, and those who serve at the altar share in the sacrificial offerings?* Paul's voluntary forgoing of the recompense for his ministry must not, however, be allowed to serve as an incentive or an excuse for being inconsiderate. The ministers of the Christian community do have a right to a livelihood from the work they perform, however gladly and willingly they expend themselves in doing it. Their generosity must not become the justification for neglect or want of liberality in those whom they serve.

9:14 *In the same way, the Lord commanded that those who proclaim the gospel should get their living by the gospel.* This command of the Lord, so far as can be determined, has no trace in the written tradition. It is one of those unwritten sayings of the Lord, an agraphon, that bears out John's hyperbole, "But there are also many other things which Jesus did; were every one of them to be written, I suppose that the world itself could not contain the books that would be written" (John 21:25). The saying, whatever its ultimate source, only enunciates an evident truth that is beyond dispute.

9:15 But I have made no use of any of these rights, nor am I writing this to secure any such provision. Lest his motive be misinterpreted, Paul assures the Corinthians that he had not availed himself of what was clearly his right; nor is he now by indirection soliciting their assistance. The astonishing charade between voluble beggars and covertly compunctious benefactors with which both history and our own times acquaint us ought to make Paul's words and the reason that prompted them quite readily comprehensible. Rarely do benefactions come without strings attached. What good is wealth if it does not confer power? And what good is power if it is not exercised?

For I would rather die than have any one deprive me of my ground for boasting. The grounds for his boasting is the freedom that is his in the Lord. Having freely given up his claim for recompense in the ministry, Paul jealously guards his reason for boasting. It is only God who gives gifts unconditionally, who sets the recipient free in the very act of donation. Practically every other gift, however ostensibly gratuitous and no matter how disinterested it claims to be, conceals fetters that bind the recipient. Ancient times provide innumerable examples of conflicts between bishops and kings. Imperial largesse hamstrung popes and church councils alike in the pursuit of their mission. Our own times furnish ample instances of initially generous donors either calling in their debts or else reneging on the gift itself when the recipient proves refractory. It is all too easy for church leaders to try to please donors by failing to speak of social ills. To give in to such a temptation would be a grave offense against the freedom about which Paul speaks.

9:16 For if I preach the gospel, that gives me no ground for boasting. For necessity is laid upon me. Woe to me if I do not preach the gospel! Paul's boast is not of the work he does but of the utter freedom with which he does it. The work itself, the preaching of the gospel, is not an option but an obligation. When the young Karl Barth first came as a new pastor to his humble village congregation, he reminded them from his Sunday pulpit, "I am not speaking of God because I am a pastor; I am a pastor because I *must* speak to you of God."

The compulsion under which Paul labors is that under which all who preach the gospel must labor. It is of the essence of the prophetic proclamation. The account of Isaiah's call to the prophetic office (Isa 6:6–10) or Jeremiah's (Jer 1:4–10) makes this amply clear. Neither had any say in undertaking the arduous task of prophesying. Jeremiah's plangent tones, already cited in connection with Paul's mission to preach the gospel (see 1 Cor 1:17), merit citing in their larger context:

> O Lord, you have enticed me, and I was enticed;
> you have overpowered me, and you have prevailed.
> I have become a laughing-stock all day long;
> everyone mocks me.
> For whenever I speak, I must cry out,
> I must shout, "Violence and destruction!"
> For the word of the Lord has become for me
> a reproach and derision all day long.
> If I say, "I will not mention him,
> or speak any more in his name,"
> then within me there is something like a burning fire
> shut up in my bones;
> I am weary with holding it in, and I cannot.
> (Jer 20:7–9 NRSV)

9:17 For if I do this of my own will, I have a reward; but if not of my own will, I am entrusted with a commission. Had the preaching of the gospel been the mere indulgence of a velleity, it would have every reason to claim its reward. Whatever the multiplicity of reasons for choosing the ministry of the Word in ages past, in our own times it has been classified and touted as a "profession" much like any other. Therefore, its candidates join of their "own will" and weigh the possibilities of "reward," however minimal. This is not to overlook for a minute the many among them who are genuinely "entrusted with a commission." In some, this commission is manifest right from the start; in others, it is awakened gradually. But the permanent obstacle in the path of both one and the other is the continuous presence in the church of those who go about preaching the gospel as a potentially lucrative profession, applying to it all the norms and criteria of those professions that they covet had they but had the ability and talent.

9:18 What then is my reward? Just this: that in my preaching I may make the gospel free of charge, not making full use of my right in the gospel. Precious as the exercise of freedom in proclaiming the gospel is, it is always beset by dangers and menaced by enemies. There is no better bulwark against these than the realization that the sovereign liberty to "make the gospel free of charge" is its own reward. To paraphrase Saint Augustine: As the reward of loving is the beloved, so too the reward of preaching the gospel is the gospel preached.

9:19 For though I am free from all men, I have made myself a slave to all, that I might win the more. Paul's concern is still freedom, his own freedom as an apostle. It is the hardest freedom to exercise, for it is free from all other men and women, their judgments, prejudices, attitudes, and standards. It requires true hardihood to keep it and genuine courage to give it expression. As a minister, Paul is not there to please the multitudes, flatter their outlook, or conform to their expectations. His service to them is a slavery to their supreme good, whether they recognize it or not. He does not minister to them from a lofty condescending eminence but as a lowly slave serving their true good. Even his servitude is an act of freedom: "I have made myself a slave to all."

It must be kept in mind, however, that this slavery is not a subservience to the demands of the multitude or a conformity to the prevalent preferences of the crowd. The exercise of this service is, and can only be, an exercise of love, "that I might win more of them" (NRSV). Anyone who has loved must know how tyrannous the beloved can sometimes be and what strength true love must exert in order to will the good of the other without compromise. This is not a popular attitude to assume. But the price of succumbing to the pressures of popularity or giving in to the emotional blackmail of the other is nothing short of relinquishing one's freedom in the ministry, and thereby forfeiting the ability to serve lovingly.

9:20 To the Jews I became as a Jew, in order to win Jews; to those under the law I became as one under the law—though not being myself under the law—that I might win those under the law. The true end of freedom in the ministry is the service of others, in their particular situation, with their specific characteristics, while being ever cautious not to wound their religious sensitivities. Even though Paul, like every other Christian (Gal 5:18; 2:16; 3:13), is no longer "under the law," he does not hesitate to act "as one under the law," as a law-abiding Jew, in order that he might the better serve the Jews and win them to Christ, even as he and his fellow apostles had been won. Those under the law are Paul's fellow Jews, and, as he says in Romans, "My heart's desire and prayer to God for them is that they may be saved" (Rom 10:1; 9:1–5).

9:21 To those outside the law I became as one outside the law—not being without law toward God but under the law of Christ—that I might win those outside the law. The catholicism of the apostle's solicitude extends to his entire world, Jews as well as Gentiles, those under the law and those outside it. In describing his attitude "as one outside the law," Paul forestalls a common enough misunderstanding. Law in this verse has two distinct senses: the prescriptive law from which all Christians are set free (Rom 6:14; 7:6); and the law of Christ, which is descriptive, the law of love in the new creation, "the law of the Spirit of life in Christ Jesus" (Rom 8:2). Fulfilling the law of Christ, the apostle becomes as one outside the law in order to win those outside the law.

9:22 To the weak I became weak, that I might win the weak. The variation on the principal theme of Paul's readiness to adapt his ministry to those he serves merely confirms the end of all apostolic labors: to win all for Christ. If the weak merit a consideration, it is by reason both of their sizeable number in any community and of the peculiarly sensitive attention they require in the exercise of the ministry. They, in particular, need to be drawn "with cords of compassion" (Hos 11:4).

I have become all things to all men, that I might by all means save some. The summary statement can readily be misconstrued as Machiavellian by all those who do not know the price it exacts from the minister. Becoming "all things to all men" requires, first of all, the arduous task of coming to know them, to know what "devours them." Moreover, it exacts from the minister the price of dying to self in order genuinely to serve the other. Mark's Gospel of discipleship sums this up in "If any man would come after me, let him deny himself and take up his cross and follow me" (Mark 8:34). Service of the other always implies death to self that the other may live. It is denying oneself—the death to oneself—that is the meaning of taking up the cross, the only way open to the disciples who follow the crucified master.

Paul, as is only fitting, is not sanguine about the prospects of his ministry. Success in it, even when it comes, is limited and precarious. The modesty of "save some" is a twofold acknowledgment both of the limitations of human endeavor and, above all, of the unfailing efficacy of God's power: "I planted, Apollos watered, but God gave the growth" (1 Cor 3:6).

9:23 I do it all for the sake of the gospel, that I may share in its blessings. The only worthy cause in the ministry is the gospel. This is an objective easily lost sight of and, consequently, ever in need of being called to the attention of the ministers. Not only is the gospel its own reward, but it brings in its wake a multiplicity of blessings. To be sure, "the laborer deserves his wages" (1 Tim 5:18). But the gospel also enables the minister to live ever more fully "under the law of Christ": "We are treated as impostors, and yet are true; as unknown, and yet well known; as dying, and behold we live; as punished, and yet not killed; as sorrowful, yet always rejoicing; as poor, yet making many rich; as having nothing, and yet possessing everything" (2 Cor 6:8–10).

9:24 *Do you not know that in a race all the runners compete, but only one receives the prize? So run that you may obtain it.* The evident appropriateness of the image in a similar context becomes heightened when addressed to Corinth, the famous locale of the Isthmian games. The almost banal truth that only the first can be number one, that first place in any endeavor is by definition unique, must strike contemporary ears as odd. Ours is the indiscriminate equality of the realm of the Wonderland Dodo, "Everybody has won, and all must have prizes." Where there is no incentive, there is no endeavor; and where there is endeavor, there is inevitable disparity of results. People's misconception of democracy, even in religious matters, leads them to confound equality with equity. We are all equal only in God's eyes; and that optic is necessarily unique. No amount of social engineering can obviate the inconvenience of this fact.

Paul's reminder of these verities is intended to rouse the indolent from their pious lethargy. Becoming a Christian is not the end of the line but the beginning of unflagging response to God's gift of grace. Being a Christian is not a license to idleness but an incentive for indefatigable service. What distinguishes the Christian metaphor of the race is that the individual runners do not look over their shoulder, but, "forgetting what lies behind and straining forward to what lies ahead," they press on "toward the goal for the prize of the upward call of God in Christ Jesus" (Phil 3:13–14).

9:25 *Every athlete exercises self-control in all things. They do it to receive a perishable wreath, but we an imperishable.* The athletic metaphor advances to the requisite self-discipline for all the entrants into the race. The privations, exertions, and fatigue they undergo for a "perishable wreath":

How vainly men themselves amaze
To win the palm, the oak, or bays
And their uncessant labours see
Crowned from some single herb or tree....
(Andrew Marvell, "The Garden")

All these are not to be compared with the "uncessant labours" of the Christian in the service of the neighbor. For the follower of Christ, there is, not the "marcescible bays" this world has to offer, but "the crown of life which God has promised to those who love him" (Jas 1:12).

9:26–27 Well, I do not run aimlessly, I do not box as one beating the air; but I pommel my body and subdue it, lest after preaching to others I myself should be disqualified. The entire life of the minister of the Word is a protracted sermon. Perhaps as much as a reminder to himself as an exhortation to the Corinthians, Paul offers himself as an example: "Be imitators of me" (1 Cor 4:16; 11:1). He knows that one of the worst risks any minister of the gospel runs is the failure to listen to the word of life that he preaches to others, forgetting that what he proclaims applies every bit as much to himself as to his hearers: "They bind heavy burdens, hard to bear, and lay them on men's shoulders; but they themselves will not move them with their finger" (Matt 23:4).

Chapter 10

FIRST CORINTHIANS 10

10:1 I want you to know, brethren, that our fathers were all under the cloud, and all passed through the sea,... Whether Paul is responding to a question put to him in the letter from Corinth or reacting to information he received from visitors who came from there, his opening words, "I want you to know," are not meant to communicate new instruction but to remind the Corinthians of what should already be familiar to them. What he does here is apply a method of interpretation in which the events of the Old Testament are seen as types of their final realization in the New. This "typology," as it is called (1 Cor 11:6; Rom 5:14), is applied here to the deliverance of Israel from their slavery in Egypt:

> And the Lord went before them by day in a pillar of cloud to lead them along the way, and by night in a pillar of fire to give them light, that they might travel by day and by night; the pillar of cloud by day and the pillar of fire by night did not depart from before the people. (Exod 13:21–22)

> And the people of Israel went into the midst of the sea on dry ground, the waters being a wall to them on their right hand and on their left. (Exod 14:22)

10:2 and all were baptized into Moses in the cloud and in the sea,... Paul is well acquainted not only with Greek rhetoric but also with the rabbinic method of interpretation known as "midrash." It is the exposition (this is the meaning of the Hebrew term) of the biblical text for the instruction of the faithful. Here, in all likelihood, Paul employs the method with a Christian twist. As he is accustomed to speak of Christians having been "baptized into Christ" (Rom 6:3), so he speaks here of the Israelites "baptized into Moses."

10:3–4 and all ate the same supernatural [NRSV: spiritual] food and all drank the same supernatural [NRSV: spiritual] drink. The Exodus narrative of the sojourn in the wilderness continues:

> Then the Lord said to Moses, "Behold, I will rain bread from heaven for you; and the people shall go out and gather a day's portion every day, that I may prove them, whether they will walk in my law or not."...And the people of Israel ate the manna forty years, till they came to a habitable land; they ate the manna, till they came to the border of the land of Canaan. (Exod 16:4, 35; Deut 8:3)

The crossing of the sea and the trek across the wilderness were, understandably enough, a focus for both Israel's and the Christian life of worship. One has only to consider this passage in Corinthians and the discourse on the bread of life in John 6 to appreciate the inexhaustible riches of Israel's history with its God (Pss 105:39–45; 78:23–29) for the nascent faith.

For they drank from the supernatural Rock [NRSV: spiritual rock] which followed them, and the Rock [NRSV: rock] was Christ. Rich and inspiring though the miracles of the exodus are, the provision of water in the wilderness must be—at least for anyone who knows the desert—the most dazzling. Even Moses, hitherto unhesitating in his obedience to the Lord, falters at this wonder:

> "Take the rod, and assemble the congregation, you and Aaron your brother, and tell the rock before their eyes to yield its water; so you shall bring water out of the rock for them; so you shall give drink to the congregation and

118

their cattle."...And Moses lifted up his hand and struck the rock with his rod twice; and water came forth abundantly, and the congregation drank, and their cattle. And the Lord said to Moses and Aaron, "Because you did not believe in me, to sanctify me in the eyes of the people of Israel, therefore you shall not bring this assembly into the land which I have given them." (Num 20:8, 11–12)

The rock in the wilderness gushes water, and the water gives life and saves. The typology of this event for the Christian was not far to seek: that rock of life and salvation is Christ. The patristic period never ceased to exploit this Exodus typology to the great enrichment of the church and its liturgy.

10:5 Nevertheless with most of them God was not pleased; for they were overthrown in the wilderness. The cause of God's displeasure with his people sets a pattern that will be repeated again and again in Israel's history. Perhaps no better sustained example of this can be found than in the Book of Judges, where the pattern of rebellion, repentance, and reconciliation recurs from one judge who ruled Israel to another. The rebellion in the desert, nevertheless, stands as a warning for all successive generations; even as Moses' plea with the Lord stands as a consolation for them:

Now if you kill this people as one man, then the nations who have heard your fame will say, "Because the Lord was not able to bring this people into the land which he swore to give to them, therefore he has slain them in the wilderness." And now, I pray you, let the power of the Lord be great as you have promised, saying, "The Lord is slow to anger, and abounding in steadfast love, forgiving iniquity and transgression." (Num 14:15–18; Ps 78:13–22)

10:6 Now these things are warnings for us, not to desire evil as they did. The wilderness years are also instructive negatively. Not only

119

are the events themselves types of divine bounty, but so too are the warnings of the constant temptations to which God's people can succumb. They served as a lesson to the Israelites; they are no less a lesson to the new creation. There is, after all, but one people of God:

> They forgot what he had done, and the miracles that
>   he had shown them.
> In the sight of their fathers he wrought marvels in the
>   land of Egypt....
> He divided the sea and let them pass through it, and
>   made the waters stand like a heap.
> In the daytime he led them with a cloud, and all the
>   night with a fiery light.
> He cleft rocks in the wilderness, and gave them drink
>   abundantly as from the deep.
> He made streams come out of the rock, and caused
>   waters to flow down like rivers.
> Yet they sinned still more against him, rebelling
>   against the Most High in the desert.
> They tested God in their heart by demanding the food
>   they craved....
> Therefore, when the Lord heard, he was full of wrath;
> a fire was kindled against Jacob, his anger mounted
>   against Israel. (Ps 78:11–21)

The temptation to "desire evil" is no less ours. It is easy to delight in the gifts and forget the giver. It is easier still to forget the utter gratuity of the gifts and come to regard them as earned and deserved, as due rights.

10:7 Do not be idolaters as some of them were; as it is written, "The people sat down to eat and drink and rose up to dance." The threat of idolatry accompanies us throughout life, whether in the substitution of ourselves for the Creator or in falling down to worship some creature or other. Spiritual writers were wont to remark that the Ten Commandments are all reducible to the first: "You shall have no other gods before me" (Exod 20:3). Every other commandment is, in its way, but an illustration of this one commandment.

Paul's recourse to Exodus 32:6 to firm his exhortation must be seen in its context to be properly understood. The people in the wilderness, their patience exhausted, ask Aaron, "Up, make us gods, who shall go before us...." When Aaron acceded to their wishes, they erected a calf of their melted gold trinkets, and said, "These are your gods, O Israel, who brought you up out of the land of Egypt!" (Exod 32:1, 4). The unforgivable enormity of their idolatrous action is the attribution of the saving deliverance from Egypt to other than the Lord their God.

Although the manufacture of idols is not a thriving industry today, their erection is. To be sure, Christians are not given to bowing their knees to inanimate objects, but they do readily bow their minds and hearts to the self-acclaimed deities that crowd the highways of modern life. Nor are all such deities secular. The world of religions is thronged with idols whose words are taken as absolute truth, whose views are determinative, whose every wish is sacred. Theologians and theologasters are kept busy furnishing tokens of their legitimacy.

10:8 We must not indulge in [NRSV: sexual] immorality as some of them did, and twenty-three thousand fell in a single day. Pace the NRSV translators, the "immorality" here is not, in the first place, sexual; for *porneia* here refers, as it often does, to the worship of idols: "You also took your fair jewels of my gold and of my silver, which I had given you, and made for yourself images of men, and with them played the harlot" (Ezek 16:17, and see Lev 17:7; Isa 23:17; Jer 3:2, 9; Hos 4:12; 5:4). The reference in this verse, both in the Hebrew and the Greek, is to *porneia*, "harlotry," of the people in the land: "While Israel dwelt in Shittim the people began to play the harlot with the daughters of Moab. These invited the people to the sacrifices of their gods, and the people ate, and bowed down to their gods" (Num 25:12).

121

10:9 We must not put the Lord to the test, as some of them did and were destroyed by serpents;... Paul proceeds with his application of Israel's wilderness experience to the church in Corinth. To "put the Lord to the test" is, of course, only by way of speaking. It uses a biblical idiom to convey the warning: "You shall not put the Lord your God to the test" (Deut 6:16; Isa 7:12; cf. Deut 8:16; 13:3; 1 Cor 3:13). It is a warning to the Corinthians not to forget their fealty and obedience to "Christ," as many of the manuscripts have here in place of "the Lord." This in itself is an astonishing phenomenon so early on: to substitute so readily "Christ" for "the Lord" in such a text, where the original Old Testament text referred to God.

10:10 nor grumble, as some of them did and were destroyed by the Destroyer. The reference is still to Israel's rebellion in the wilderness:

> And the whole congregation of the people of Israel murmured against Moses and Aaron in the wilderness, and said to them, "Would that we had died by the hand of the Lord in the land of Egypt, when we sat by the flesh-pots and ate bread to the full; for you have brought us out into this wilderness to kill this whole assembly with hunger." (Exod 16:2–3; 15:24; 17:3; Num 14:2, 29; 16:41; Deut 1:27)

It is important to keep in mind that the whole complaint is about food, and this is the context in which Paul's exhortation will be formulated (1 Cor 10:14–17; 11:20–22). The puzzle in the present text is why the RSV, which is usually so careful to preserve the same English vocable for its Old Testament equivalent, departed from "murmur" and chose "grumble," to say nothing of the NRSV's choice of "complain." Not that this matters much for the sense in the present instance, but in our times of biblical concordances and dictionaries, such inconsistency can be a hindrance.

10:11 Now these things happened to them as a warning, but they were written down for our instruction, upon whom the end of the ages has come. Two traits in Paul's exegesis of the text of the Old Testament stand out. The first is the typology, of which mention was made earlier in 1 Corinthians 10:1, where the events of Israel's history with God serve as a key to understanding those of the new creation, "for our instruction."

The second trait is Paul's eschatology, his lucid recognition of the fact that, in Christ Jesus, the new aeon, "the end of the ages," has come. The recognition of the fact that the believers are now a new creation is the determinative factor in his reading of the Bible. Many nowadays seek to dismiss this and, for reasons of their own, to insist that in Christ Jesus nothing has changed. Were this so, then Christians are the most to be pitied of creatures on the face of the earth.

10:12 *Therefore let any one who thinks that he stands take heed lest he fall.* In the first flush of that confidence that Christ's victory inspires, in the exhilaration that the good news is bound to bring to all those who sat "in darkness and in the shadow of death" (Luke 1:79), the believers can, understandably, forget their vulnerability and overlook all the dangers that surround them. There is, as G. K. Chesterton remarked, only one way to stand erect, but a thousand ways to fall. The believer cannot stand erect by his effort alone, but he is at risk of falling unaided at any moment. Paul's warning to the Corinthians was timely then. It is no less timely to each believer today.

10:13 *No temptation has overtaken you that is not common to man.* Such serenity was bound not to last, and the rest of Paul's correspondence (2 Corinthians, Galatians, Philippians) bears testimony to its disintegration. In the ordinary course of events, when the waters are calm and the wind propitious, the believer sails smoothly, her or his confidence swelling imperceptibly into overconfidence and a foolhardy disregard of all perils. Christians who lived in the years after World War II need this reminder most. They must have experienced the confidence that bordered on hubris in their life in the church. Alas, there was then no Paul to remind them that no temptation had "overtaken them that is not common to man." The believers, in their grand variety, acquiesced in the draconian measures that were the will of God, or else "grumbled" good-humoredly, hoping thereby to save their souls.

God is faithful, and he will not let you be tempted beyond your strength, but with the temptation will also provide the way of escape, that you may be able to endure it. The value of this reminder can best be appreciated after the fact, after the storm has abated, the waves subsided, and the winds calmed down. It takes rare powers of discernment in the preachers of the Word and a ready ear on the part of their hearers to appreciate the fidelity of God, who can be trusted not to let his faithful be overwhelmed and, at the opportune time, to provide them with "the way to escape."

It is by no means easy to recognize the situation at which we now stand, whether the worst of the crisis is over or yet to come, whether God's way to escape is still hidden or descried from afar by those who have the care of guiding the community of believers out of the impenetrable darkness of the storm. It is not yet evident that any such escape from the church's predicament exists. When storms like the present ones rage, the recipe for survival is there clear for all to see in the Acts of the Apostles: "And fearing that we might run on the rocks, they let out four anchors from the stern, and prayed for day to come" (27:29). But this too is impracticable. It requires the stillness of contemplation in a tumultuous world urged by its media to clamor for action.

10:14 Therefore, my beloved, shun the worship of idols. This reiterates 10:8, "We must not indulge in immorality." So, too, does the First Letter of John conclude, "Little children, keep yourselves from idols" (1 John 5:21). To us, such exhortation seems otiose; the idols have been overthrown and the gods have departed centuries ago. To the Corinthians, who knew well enough the attraction of the idols they left behind when they "turned to God from idols, to serve a living and true God" (1 Thess 1:9), this was a much-needed reminder. Old attachments die hard. Pious practices perdure. It took Christianity a long time to secure the unswerving fidelity of the believers to Christ and to assume and transmute old pieties into Christian ritual.

The process has never really ceased. To be sure, the names of the idols have changed and the nature of the pious practices altered. But the community of believers has always stood in need of this imperative to "shun the worship of idols," whether racial, national, ethnic, or personal.

A brief remark on Paul's mode of address, "my beloved," is called for here. This is no empty title of courtesy. Paul genuinely loves the Corinthians (1 Cor 4:14; 15:58; 2 Cor 7:1; 12:19), as he does all the communities he serves (1 Thess 2:7, 11; Gal 4:19; Phil 4:1). Indeed, it can be said without fear of contradiction that without this love no true Christian ministry is possible. You cannot minister to those you don't love. "My beloved" is merely a reminder of that fact.

10:15 I speak as to sensible men; judge for yourselves what I say. All the previous biblical interpretation of the events of Israel in the wilderness (10:1–14) was a preparation for this. Paul's choice of the incidents which had to do with food and drink must surely have had the Lord's Supper in view. His appeal to the Corinthians as "sensible men" is matter of fact and not just a rhetorical *captatio benevolentiae*, an attempt at winning their good will.

Teachers and instructors, leaders and ministers in the church, usually show little partiality for the "judge for yourselves" part of this verse. Whether it be mistrust of the intelligence of the believers or jealous safeguarding of their own authority, the net result, whatever the appearances, is a loss of confidence and—increasingly in our day—cynicism. The God who conferred intelligence on the ministers of the Word did not withhold it from those to whom they minister. Indeed, without intelligence, faith and the teaching of the faith can only be superstition.

10:16 The cup of blessing which we bless, is it not a participation [koinōnia: communion] in the blood of Christ? As he had under-

125

taken an interpretation of the exodus event (1 Cor 10:1–13), so now Paul theologizes on a tradition of the new exodus. In a world full of theological methods and methodologies, it is instructive, not to say illuminating, to observe the apostle set about the task of theologizing on the tradition of the Lord's Supper. He displays an admirable example of theology as a discourse on the given of the faith. He takes the cup first, not to alter the usual order of bread first and then the cup, but to allow him to expatiate on the bread at greater length. So, the reason for the inversion of the order is not ritual but merely stylistic.

The "cup of blessing" in the Lord's Supper is, in Paul's theological optic, a "communion," really the best English word to render the Greek *koinōnia*, whence we also have, significantly enough in the context, "community." To be sure, the Greek term can be rendered "participation" (RSV) or "sharing" (NRSV), but it is most suitably rendered by "communion," with its cognate of "community" and its connotation of "union," however the pseudo-sophisticates among today's Christians may shun it for no other reason than that they once received "holy communion."

The theological significance of the cup is precisely the union it effects between the believer and the death of Christ on the cross. The reference to blood, here and elsewhere in Paul, is to the death of Christ on the cross (Rom 3:25; 5:9; 1 Cor 11:25, 27). The only way the believer has access to redemption and eternal life is in the cross of Jesus. All the sacraments (see Rom 6:3) draw their efficacy from the contact they effect with this central mystery of the death of Christ; and prime among them is the Eucharist.

Two remarks are called for here. Whenever Paul speaks of the blood, the cross, the death on the cross, he refers to the Christ event in its entirety, namely, to the life, death and resurrection of Jesus Christ. Furthermore, Paul spoke of the Lord's Supper, not of the "Eucharist" (Greek *eucharistia*), which term had to await Saint Ignatius of Antioch at the end of the first century for its currency. The verb "to give thanks" (Greek *eucharistein*) is, of course, used by Paul and the rest of the New Testament. The account of the institution of the Eucharist says that Jesus "blessed" (Mark 14:22; Matt 26:26; Luke 24:30) and/or "gave thanks" (Mark 14:23; Matt 26:27; Luke 22:17, 19; 1 Cor 11:24). The former, "blessed," is the Hebrew form of the expression, the latter, "gave thanks," is the Greek. So, as we have here, the cup of blessing is simply the eucharistic cup.

The bread which we break, is it not a participation in the body of Christ? The "body" here is, of course, "my body which is for you" (1 Cor 11:24, 27). Its referent is the "Lord's death" (11:26). In other words, Paul continues his theologizing on the datum of the eucharistic tradition. Partaking of this body is a communion in the redeeming death of Christ. The profundity of Paul's theological insight here is often overlooked in the centuries-old controversies on the mystery of the Lord's Supper. So far as the available evidence allows, Paul stands out as the first theologian of the Eucharist. No small distinction!

10:17 Because there is one bread, we who are many are one body, for we all partake of the one bread. Communion in the Body of Christ is taken one theological step further: It is the agent of unity in the Body of Christ. Here Paul uses "body of Christ" in two distinct senses: the "body for you" in the Lord's Supper, and the "body of Christ" that the community (*koinōnia*) of believers is, "Now you are the body of Christ" (1 Cor 12:27). This dual meaning of the term, by the way, is the reason why "Body of Christ" remains the prime designation of the church even after Vatican II.

Participation in the "one bread" reduces the multiplicity and diversity of believers to the unity of the Body of Christ, not to uniformity. The cogency of Paul's theological insight is only heightened when we consider the tragedy of the present rupture and division in the Christian community.

Barely fifty years after the apostle wrote these words, the *Didache*, a manual of Christian instruction, elaborated the image of the bread and unity in another direction:

As this broken bread was scattered upon the mountains
and being gathered together became one, so may your
Church be gathered together from the ends of the earth
into your kingdom. (*Didache* IX.4)

*10:18 Consider the people of Israel; are not those who eat the sac-
rifices partners in the altar?* Paul has not quit the events of God's
holy people in the wilderness. He recalls here an almost evident
fact. Those who eat of the sacrifice offered on the altar are partners, participants, communicants (*koinōnoi*) "in the altar." In
other words, there is some visible means for the individual
believer to come in contact with the divinity. Howsoever trivial-
ized the image may be in our day, sitting at table, sharing a meal,
remains a powerful expression of communion.

*10:19 What do I imply then? That food offered to idols is anything,
or that an idol is anything?* This is the mark of the conscientious
correspondent. Paul hastens to forestall any misunderstanding on
the point he made in chapter 8, "concerning food offered to idols"
(1 Cor 8:1). What he says about participation in the sacrifice
offered at the altar in no way affirms the existence of idols (8:4).
The Corinthian church had its share, as does today's church, of
believers ready to leap at the least loophole in an argument to provide them with the means to avoid its undesirable implications.
Sophistry is a powerful instrument of evasion in the hand of shirk-
ers in any generation.

*10:20 No, I imply that what pagans sacrifice they offer to demons
and not to God. I do not want you to be partners with demons.* The
situation of Christians in Corinth was far from simple. The discussion of food offered to idols in a previous section of the letter
(1 Cor 8) was concerned with scandal and edification of the weak
by the strong in the community. Here, however, Paul is concerned
with the perils to which all Christians are exposed in a pagan
milieu. His world contained evil powers and demons that were no
less real to him than to his readers. The warning can as well be

addressed to today's Christians who, although they live in an ostensibly non-pagan world, are no less exposed to evil powers and demonic forces, which are all the more dangerous for not being spiritual and for not being recognized for what they are.

10:21–22 *You cannot drink the cup of the Lord and the cup of demons. You cannot partake of the table of the Lord and the table of demons. Shall we provoke the Lord to jealousy? Are we stronger than he?* A necessary reminder to all fence straddlers, whether in Corinth's world or in ours. The tags and labels change, but the items remain the same. Faith in demons may be passé; anthropomorphisms like provoking "the Lord to jealousy" may not be a popular idiom; but temptations to look for salvation elsewhere than in the cross of Jesus Christ, howsoever you may wish to designate them, are a genuine and abiding peril. You may wish to call preaching against such ersatz soteriologies bigotry, intolerance, political incorrectness, or what have you. Paul's reminder remains, nevertheless, ever urgent. You simply cannot "drink the cup of the Lord and the cup of demons," however liberal, postmodern, or democratic it be to do so.

10:23 *"All things are lawful," but not all things are helpful. "All things are lawful," but not all things build up.* We have come, as it were, full circle. The Corinthian slogan of individual freedom, "All things are lawful," "I am free to do anything" (REB), "Every thing is lawful for me" (NABRE) (1 Cor 6:12), is here repeated twice, and both times, far from being denied, is distinguished. However surprising it may seem, everything is allowed, all is permitted to the Christian. The believer is under no restraint. Far from denying this fundamental freedom of the Christian, Paul introduces a distinction that puts the full onus of the exercise of this freedom squarely on the believer. As we saw earlier in the section on "food offered to idols," what sets bounds to, what defines the exercise of Christian freedom, is always the other, the neighbor, the brother.

"All things are lawful" to be sure; but I have to keep in mind that some things can be a hindrance, a stumbling block, not helpful to the other. In the exercise of my freedom I have to keep in mind always "the brother for whom Christ died" (1 Cor 8:11). I must forever be on the alert lest the use of my freedom wound or destroy (8:12, 11) my brother. This is the negative side of the distinction qualifying "All things are lawful."

But there is a positive, a more onerous aspect that must be kept in mind. The exercise of my liberty must be careful not only not to harm and destroy, but it must also look to building up, to edifying the other. The grace of Christian freedom, like all graces, brings with it obligation: the obligation of vigilance lest I cause harm to the other, and the even more exigent obligation to use this gift to build up, to edify the other in the Body of Christ.

10:24 Let no one seek his own good, but the good of his neighbor. For no readily perceptible reason, the NRSV translates, "Do not seek your own advantage, but that of the other." The Greek original is, in its simplicity ("yours" and "the other's"), more inclusive. However you may wish to translate it, the verse makes explicit the two distinctions brought to bear on "All things are lawful" in the previous verse. The burden of the believer's freedom falls squarely on the one who exercises it. Whatever past pastoral practice may have led us to believe, there is no evasion of this responsibility by applying to ecclesiastical powers for exemptions, suspensions, or exceptions. The rule of Christian life is simple in the extreme: Look to the good of the other, not to your own. No one has ever said that being a Christian is easy. But it is extremely simple, despite all the efforts of ecclesiastics, theologians, and moralists to complicate it.

10:25 Eat whatever is sold in the meat market without raising any question on the ground of conscience. This, at least, Christians have usually followed almost unquestioningly. Moral theologians have found little purchase here. Haste in judgment, however, would be ill advised. With current problems of obesity and raised awareness of animal rights, it won't be long before moral picadors will descend into the arena, and Christians will have yet another righteous cause to deflect their attention from the gospel.

10:26 For "the earth is the Lord's, and everything in it." Recourse to the Scriptures (Pss 24:1; 50:12; 89:11) in this instance is only a natural reminder of the Creator's dominion over all creation. It is, consequently, a reminder that "whatever is sold in the meat market" is a gift and must be treated accordingly. This is by no means an unnecessary reminder in a world where glut and famine exist side by side. It is all the more urgent, therefore, for the believers who happen to be in the midst of plenty not to seek their own good but the good of their neighbor (1 Cor 10:24).

10:27 If one of the unbelievers invites you to dinner and you are disposed to go, eat whatever is set before you without raising any question on the ground of conscience. This advice is an example of Paul's pastoral common sense and pastoral sensitivity. Would that Christians would always have this kind of flexibility regarding harmless customs and manners.

10:28–29 (But if some one says to you, "This has been offered in sacrifice," then out of consideration for the man who informed you, and for conscience' sake—I mean his conscience, not yours—do not eat it.) For why should my liberty be determined by another man's scruples? It is hard to think that a remark of that "some one" about the food having been offered to idols could have been made without ill will. Such remarks, more often than not, are malicious. Everyone in Corinth must have known that there was no meat to be had in that city that had not been offered to idols. The enormous number of sacrifices and ordinary economic sense would have seen to that.

Consideration of the weak in the community always demands patience and longsuffering. The weak, by and large, are insufferable. Hence, the need for Paul's reminder here and in 1 Corinthians 8:9–13. The Christian exercise of liberty is made all the costlier by the preponderance of the weak of every variety in the Christian community. Paul echoes the question of anyone who tries to exercise Christian freedom responsibly: "For why should my liberty be determined by another man's scruples?" Why indeed?

10:30 If I partake with thankfulness, why am I denounced because of that for which I give thanks? The eminently good sense here was destined for neglect. Provided I receive God's gifts with gratitude, what business is it of anyone, high or low in the community, to pass judgment on me? This is so inescapably commonsensical that one wonders how, for centuries, it has been relegated to almost utter oblivion.

10:31 So, whether you eat or drink, or whatever you do, do all to the glory of God. This is a perfect, compendious, and all-embracing summary of what Paul has been saying thus far. Receiving all and everything from the hand of the Creator with gratitude is what giving glory to God means. It avoids the sin of sins in Christian life: divorcing the gifts from their Giver, mistaking the utter largesse of the Giver for a right of the recipient. This is why gratitude is at the heart of Christian life; and the Eucharist its abiding memorial.

10:32–33 Give no offense to Jews or to Greeks or to the church of God, just as I try to please all men in everything I do, not seeking my own advantage, but that of many, that they may be saved. This can almost go without saying, yet said it must be. My responsibility in the exercise of my liberty extends to everyone who crosses my path, Jews or Greeks or the church of God. Seeking the advantage of the other, "the good of his neighbor" (1 Cor 10:24), that he or she "may be saved" is the task of every Christian on earth. It is not my business how they are saved. But everything I do must be done with their salvation in view. This is what it means to seek the good of the other, what loving the other means.

To "please all men in everything I do" says no more than recognizing in every single one of those whom I encounter, even under the most banal of circumstances of life, "the brother for whom Christ died" (8:11). Every liturgy we attend reminds us of this one fact, that Christ shed his blood for all, without cavil, without exception.

Chapter 11

FIRST CORINTHIANS 11

11:1 Be imitators of me, as I am of Christ. The verse serves as a conclusion to the previous section rather than the beginning of this new one. It repeats what Paul had said already in 1 Corinthians 4:16, "Be imitators of me," only adding here "as I am of Christ." The theme is common enough in Pauline literature: "Brethren, join in imitating me, and mark those who so live as you have an example in us" (Phil 3:17); "What you have learned and received and heard and seen in me, do" (4:9); "And you became imitators of us and of the Lord" (1 Thess 1:6). Perhaps Second Thessalonians sums it up best when it has Paul saying that what he did was "to give you in our conduct an example to imitate" (2 Thess 3:9). Every minister of the Word should have the courage to say this, because the whole life of the minister ought to be one uninterrupted sermon.

Yet there are those who delight in dislodging Paul from his pedestal and regard this statement as encouraging a cult of personality. Before doing so, however, let them consider that "Be imitators of me" can just as well be an invitation to share the paradoxes of the apostle's life in the ministry: foolish, in weakness, in disrepute, in hunger and thirst, "ill-clad and buffeted and homeless," reviled, persecuted, slandered, "the refuse of the world, the offscouring of all things" (1 Cor 4:10–13); "through great endurance, in afflictions, hardships, calamities, beatings, imprisonments, tumults, labors, watching, hunger" (2 Cor 6:4–5). If this be the stuff of personality cults, let's have more of it.

11:2 I commend you because you remember me in everything and maintain the traditions even as I have delivered them to you. The life of the apostle is by no means unrelieved gloom amid successive catastrophes. Paul has much reason to rejoice in the Corinthians' fidelity to the gospel tradition he delivered to them. He realized, as those who came after him often chose not to, that, as has been remarked, "the force of Christian tradition is not coercive." This is why he "commends" the Corinthians. Time and time again, the subsequent centuries will show coercion to be the mark of counterfeit tradition. People accept the faith. They cannot be compelled into it, either by main force or by logical argument.

11:3 But I want you to understand that the head of every man is Christ, the head of a woman is her husband, and the head of Christ is God. Paul enunciates this hierarchic principle to prepare the ground for dealing with yet another problem in Corinth, but one more peculiar to that time and place. Hierarchy, for Paul, is a principle of order, not of subordination. Who, for instance, in his right mind would accuse Paul's Christology of being "subordinationist," that is, asserting the Son to be inferior to the Father, when he says, "The head of Christ is God"? But this has never deterred some from accusing him of misogyny or worse when he says, "The head of a woman is her husband." Before making such accusation, one should pause to ask what it means for Christ to be "the head of every man" and then draw the appropriate analogy for man being "the head of woman." If Christ, the head of every man, loved us and gave himself up for us (Gal 2:20), could "the head of woman" be expected to do less?

11:4–6 Any man who prays or prophesies with his head covered dishonors his head, but any woman who prays or prophesies with her head unveiled dishonors her head—it is the same as if her head were shaven. For if a woman will not veil herself, then she should cut off her hair; but if it is disgraceful for a woman to be shorn or shaven, let her wear a veil. The logic of this argument eludes me. Paul is defending what must have been a standing custom in his communities: men praying and prophesying with their heads uncovered, and women with their heads veiled. His desire to preserve a legitimate enough custom is comprehensible, even if the reasons he gives for it are not.

11:7–10 For a man ought not to cover his head, since he is the image and glory of God; but woman is the glory of man. (For man was not made from woman, but woman from man. Neither was man created for woman, but woman for man.) That is why a woman ought to have a veil on her head, because of the angels. Equally incomprehensible are the additional arguments Paul amasses in trying to justify an existing custom that, evidently, he cherished. In what must have been for him an extreme measure of desperation, he adds, "because of the angels," whatever that may mean. Being an apostle does not exempt you from a perfectly human trait, the desire to defend a position you hold dear, even if you hold it irrationally. Being included in the canon of the New Testament does not guarantee the strict logic of all the arguments adduced in favor of this or that proposition. What must baffle the reader in all this is how later generations read such passages on a par with Paul's proclamation, say, of Christology, of grace, of ecclesiology; or, worse still, how they understood the passage to require paper napkin head covers for women entering a church. Yet all such oddities require is utter insouciance of the fact that the New Testament is not, and was never meant to be, that sort of book.

11:11–12 (Nevertheless, in the Lord woman is not independent of man nor man of woman; for as woman was made from man, so man is now born of woman. And all things are from God.) The questionable parentheses, which open and close these two verses in the RSV, are not in the NRSV, nor is there any hint of them in the Greek text. What they state, however, is unquestionable. One would have thought that, far from furnishing a negative criticism of Paul, the mutuality of dependence between man and woman are the best argument against Paul's purported misogyny. The solemnity of "in the Lord," that is, in the Christian context, and the affirmation of the mutual dependence between women and men opened a new chapter in a world that hitherto insisted on the inequality and disparity between them. That subsequent generations paid scant attention to Paul's affirmation is not to be laid at Paul's door.

"And all things are from God" crowns the statement with the opening item of our Creed, that God is the Creator "from whom are all things and for whom we exist" (1 Cor 8:6). The interdependence of women and men is from God, not from social engineering.

11:13–15 Judge for yourselves; is it proper for a woman to pray to God with her head uncovered? Does not nature itself teach you that for a man to wear long hair is degrading to him, but if a woman has long hair, it is her pride? For her hair is given to her for a covering. The parentheses inserted by the RSV for verses 11–12 find their justification in this reversion to the argument that anteceded them. Evidently, they were inserted into the text of the RSV as an attempt at interpretation. But, then, so is every translation of the text of the New Testament, a fact that is often lost sight of in our use of these versions.

Of course, Paul's series of rhetorical questions expected affirmative responses from his readers in Corinth. Evidently, he and they shared many customs in common. Their views on such matters as the uncovered heads of women at prayer, or on men wearing their hair long, or on women's long hair, happened to coincide with Paul's own views. The sixth canon of the Council of Nicaea (325) urged the preservation of old customs; and this is what Paul is trying to do. Yet Saint Cyprian, the bishop of Carthage († 258), did not hesitate to remind his people that customs without truth are merely old falsehoods. Our views on such matters as head covering do not coincide with Paul's, and that is all there is to it. The gospel did not come to alter national customs or to provide a manual of morals for hairdressers, nor to hint at remedies for alopecia.

11:16 If any one is disposed to be contentious, we recognize no other practice, nor do the churches of God. There must have been in Corinth, as there are in every church and in every age, those who, for reasons of their own, chose to depart from the general custom. The desire of some "to be contentious," as Paul puts it, has always been merely a curiosity and not a surprising phenomenon at that. Our present age should be the very last to evince surprise at aberrant customs, styles, and modes of deportment.

Paul here is not hurling anathemas at the wayward. Oddities are fissile. He is doing all that one can do under the circumstances: affirming his own position and showing it to be one he shares with "the churches of God." His aim is to prevent the fragmentation of the community, not to eradicate a human tendency.

11:17 But in the following instructions I do not commend you, because when you come together it is not for the better but for the worse. This alteration between matters of minor import and those of extreme importance is good rhetorical practice. The switch to a new set of "instructions," which are far more than expressions of opinions and personal preferences, could not have been done more adroitly. Report of abuses in the Christian assemblies came to Paul's attention by word of mouth that reached him from Corinth ("I hear" in 11:18).

The contrast between the "I commend you" (1 Cor 11:2) of the previous section and the "I do not commend you" of this can only draw attention to the gravity of the situation that has required the apostle's instruction. Ears better attuned to oral communication than ours would not have missed the nuance when First Corinthians was read to them, as all Paul's epistles were to the early, less literate, generations of Christians. That is why rhetorical devices played a much greater role in ancient compositions than they did later when literacy was more widespread.

11:18 For, in the first place, when you assemble as a church, I hear that there are divisions among you; and I partly believe it,... That there were divisions in Corinth we already know from the opening section of the epistle.

137

For it has been reported to me by Chloe's people that there is quarreling among you, my brethren. What I mean is that each one of you says, "I belong to Paul," or "I belong to Apollos," or "I belong to Cephas," or "I belong to Christ." Is Christ divided? Was Paul crucified for you? Or were you baptized in the name of Paul? (1:11–13)

But the situation here is much graver. The division (the Greek word is *schisma*) takes place when they "assemble as a church," that is, when they come together to celebrate the Lord's Supper. We must never lose sight of the fact that the Christian community is never more "church" than when it gathers together to celebrate the Eucharist. The division, schism, that occurred in such assemblies in Corinth is so grievous as to be barely credible. Yet, realist that he is, Paul tells them, "I partly believe it."

11:19 for there must be factions among you in order that those who are genuine among you may be recognized. The reason that Paul partly believes the report is precisely his realism. The Christian community is not made up of angels, nor is its existence unearthly. When Paul says, "There must be factions among you," he is simply constating a fact, not prescribing it. He is aware of the ways of God with his people. Such divisions and tribulations as beset the community are not unmelanged evils. In Paul's Christian perspective, they are there to test us. Even the most cynical among us must acknowledge that such trials and tribulations in the Christian community often reveal the genuine items among its members. Despite all the media's glorification of those who foment such divisions and factions, the true believers are bound to discern who among them are the true followers of "Christ and him crucified." After all, those who attend eucharistic assemblies to worship Jesus Christ as Lord hardly ever attract the camera. The media seem to lack even the elementary vocabulary to describe what these worshipers are about.

11:20 When you meet together, it is not the Lord's supper that you eat. This statement is bound to baffle modern readers for whom the celebration of the Eucharist has few, clearly defined, specific requirements. It baffles them all the more for its unfamiliarity. In Paul's Corinth what occasioned the judgment that the celebration was "not the Lord's supper" was neither a deficiency in the presider, nor a defect in the elements, nor a question about the validity of the formulae employed. It had to do, rather, with the conduct of the community members themselves, assembled as a church (11:18).

11:21 For in eating, each one goes ahead with his own meal, and one is hungry and another is drunk. We need to visualize better the situation that gave rise to the problem, for it is not one that is easily familiar to us. The place of gathering was, in all likelihood, a house church, the home of one of the Christian families in Corinth, such as "the household of Stephanas" (1:16), or the church in the house of Aquila and Prisca (16:19), where the hosts themselves presided. We must also keep in mind that the evening repast and the Lord's Supper were linked (11:25).

Paul uses the term *church* in three different ways: first, the house church, as in the two instances just cited, and of which there is question here; second, the local church, "the church of God which is at Corinth" (1:2; 2 Cor 1:1) or "the church of the Thessalonians" (1 Thess 1:1); and, third, the universal church, "the church of God" (1 Cor 10:33; 6:4; 11:22; 12:28). Every one of these categories is church in the fullest sense possible. One is not more church than another. The people of Corinth were not wont to commit our vulgar error of imagining church to be either an elaborately structured church or an urban church of later centuries such as the church of Rome. The smallest church in the remotest mountain fastness with the most flea-ridden congregation is every bit as much church as the greatest cathedral in Christendom.

What prompted Paul to judge that this particular church of Corinth was not celebrating the Lord's Supper was the conduct of its heterogeneous members. There were the well-off masters, the rich slave owners, who came at their leisure, as the whim struck them, well before the start of the celebration. There were the servants and slaves of such masters, the tutors of their children, the laborers on their estates, the maids in their homes. Their arrival was dictated by the tasks they had to accomplish before they could attend. There was also, for lack of a better term, the riffraff of a great city like Corinth, the down-and-out of its society, and all those people who came "from somewhere that they were not in a hurry to go back to." They all gathered on equal footing, as brothers and sisters, the rich and the poor, the mighty and the low, all came to sing, as that famed report of the younger Pliny to the Roman emperor put it, "a hymn to Jesus Christ as to God," that is, to celebrate the Lord's Supper.

What happened was that the early arrivals started eating and drinking and getting drunk while waiting for the tired, hungry, and bedraggled latecomers to join the assembly. What ruined the Lord's Supper was not—as the sociologically minded pretend nowadays—the lack of generosity on the part of the rich or their neglect of the poor. What happened was infinitely more reprehensible and, in a Christian context, unforgivable.

11:22 What! Do you not have houses to eat and drink in? Or do you despise the church of God and humiliate those who have nothing? What shall I say to you? Shall I commend you in this? No, I will not. The grievance is not their eating and drinking. They can do as much of that as they wish in their own homes. What is at issue here is that their eating and drinking, the vulgar disporting of their possessions and of the abundance of their goods, inevitably humiliates "those who have nothing." This might seem almost incomprehensible to us who enjoy such superfluity of goods. We never stop to reflect how humiliating it is to parade our abundance before those who are in perpetual want. We pretend not to understand how even our generosity can be humiliating to the objects of our charity. Most of the rich and mighty of this world seem unable to grasp the simple fact that, as the Roman poet Ovid put it, it requires genius to give, a genius singularly lacking among the affluent of the world.

Paul began his instruction on the abuses in the Christian assembly with "I do not commend you" (11:17). He concludes it similarly with an "I will not" commend you. Once again, this is a rhetorical device to signal the beginning and end of what, in a written document, is easily recognized as a paragraph. The device of *inclusio* is all the more useful when a message is heard rather than read. In the present context it also sets the stage for the perfect antidote to the abuse: a solemn reminder to the Corinthians of what it is they come together to do when they assemble as a church to celebrate the supper of the Lord.

11:23–24 For I received from the Lord what I also delivered to you, that the Lord Jesus on the night when he was betrayed The opening formula of "received...delivered" is the tradition formula par excellence. It is precisely in that act of receiving and handing on that Christian tradition is constituted and lives. What makes it specifically Christian is that it is "from the Lord." Its ultimate source is the Lord, that is, the risen Jesus, whose specific title of glory is "the Lord." The Lord is thus not only the source of the tradition but the guarantor of its authenticity. Its universal validity derives from the immediacy of its source.

In handing on the tradition of the institution of the Lord's Supper, Paul insists on its indissoluble link with the passion: "on the night when he was betrayed." The whole understanding of the Eucharist is centered in the death of Jesus on the cross for us. It is the death on the cross that makes us who we are and what we are.

took bread, and when he had given thanks, he broke it, and said, "This is my body which is for you. Do this in remembrance of me." The phrase, "when he had given thanks," is in the Greek *eucharistēsas*, whence we now have the word *eucharist* when we speak of what Paul called the Lord's Supper. Such act of giving thanks, or blessing, is the usual Jewish piety before breaking bread and partaking of a meal.

"This is my body which is for you" is a clear and unambiguous reference to the death of Jesus on the cross: "for you." The entire intelligibility of the act is in the Christ event, which in Paul always embraces the passion, the death and the resurrection of Jesus. This is why he says, "I received from the Lord," that is, from the risen Lord. The link between the "body for you" and the Lord cannot be severed.

"Do this is remembrance of me" is the imperative to keep this tradition alive down the ages. It is by remembering that the tradition lives and, in it, the Lordship of Jesus Christ (11:26). This is why in our obedience to this injunction, we preface our eucharistic celebration with the Liturgy of the Word, our act of remembrance.

11:25 In the same way also the cup, after supper, saying, "This cup is the new covenant in my blood. Do this, as often as you drink it, in remembrance of me." The Lord's Supper was evidently celebrated in the context of the community meal, "after supper." The interpretation of the cup is in terms of the covenant that God made with his people Israel:

> Then [Moses] took the book of the covenant, and read
> it in the hearing of the people; and they said, "All that
> the Lord has spoken we will do, and we will be obedi-
> ent." And Moses took the blood and threw it upon the
> people, and said, "Behold the blood of the covenant
> which the Lord has made with you in accordance with
> all these words." (Exod 24:7–8)

Then, it was the turn of Jeremiah the prophet to proclaim a "new covenant":

> Behold, the days are coming, says the Lord, when I will
> make a new covenant with the house of Israel and the

house of Judah....But this is the covenant which I will make with the house of Israel after those days, says the Lord: I will put my law within them, and I will write it upon their hearts; and I will be their God, and they shall be my people. (Jer 31:31, 33)

The formula of the eucharistic institution in Paul now definitively identifies this new covenant with the death of Christ on the cross, the shedding of his blood for us. "Blood" in Paul is by way of being an abbreviated reference to the entire Christ event, that is, the passion, death and resurrection (Rom 3:25; 5:9; 1 Cor 10:16).

The injunction to "do this...in remembrance of me" is repeated. It keeps before us the fact that remembrance is the begetter of gratitude. Every time we remember the saving event of Christ Jesus, we give thanks, in Greek *eucharistein*, eucharist.

Over the centuries debates raged and decrees multiplied on whether receiving communion was to be under one or both species. The height of absurdity was reached when receiving the bread was conceded to *hoi polloi* and the wine was reserved to *hoi aristoi*. Reading First Corinthians ought to have put paid to the debate: eating the bread is as integral an action as drinking the cup. Consuming one or the other or both of the elements is always "in remembrance" of him who died to save us, not to segregate us.

11:26 For as often as you eat this bread and drink the cup, you proclaim the Lord's death until he comes. It is eating and drinking that is the eucharistic act. Participation in the body and blood of the Lord is what puts us in contact with the redemptive act of Jesus Christ. The act of eating and drinking is an act of proclamation of the redemptive death, an act of faith in the death for our sins (1 Cor 15:3). Indeed, all the sacraments are, each in its way, a mode of proclaiming the Word. But the Eucharist is that mode par excellence.

We have had occasion to recall how eschatology is never far from Paul's mind. It should not be far from ours either. The repeated proclamation of the Christ event, of the death of the Lord, is "until he comes." Every Eucharist is a reminder of this fact. The church's liturgy, with unerring judgment, places the Our Father immediately before eating the bread and drinking the cup. The community always prays before communion, "Your kingdom come." But it should never forget that this can come to pass only when "Your will be done." The Lord's express will is for us to "do this in remembrance of me."

11:27 Whoever, therefore, eats the bread or drinks the cup of the Lord in an unworthy manner will be guilty of profaning the body and blood of the Lord. At the start of this instruction on the Lord's Supper, Paul had to call the attention of the Corinthians to the fact that "when you meet together, it is not the Lord's supper that you eat" (11:20). Here he goes on to explain the reason why: You must come together as the Body of Christ in order to eat the body of Christ. If you don't, then "it is not the Lord's supper that you eat." By humiliating those who have nothing (11:22), they ceased to be the Body of Christ and, therefore, did not eat the Lord's Supper. The wonder of the mystery is simply this: If they come to the Lord's Supper as the body of Christ, they become the Body of Christ by eating it. The circularity of the statement is precisely the mystery. This is why now Paul puts the full weight of responsibility on each participant in the Lord's Supper, and certainly not on rubrics or canonical directives.

The judgment of the worthy or unworthy manner in which each "eats the bread or drinks the cup of the Lord" belongs to the individual believer. Each passes judgment on herself or himself. The care and responsibility each one bears in seeing to it that he or she come to the Lord's Supper as a member of the Body of Christ is neither transmissible nor extensible to others. This is one reason why our liturgies are prefaced by a penitential rite, to ask pardon for our sins.

11:28 Let a man examine himself, and so eat of the bread and drink of the cup. Paul's meaning is clear. The onus falls squarely on each woman and man who eats the bread and drinks the cup. The personal responsibility is unequivocal. It can neither be ceded by the member of the Body of Christ, nor arrogated by another, however lofty his position on the ladder.

11:29 For any one who eats and drinks without discerning the body eats and drinks judgment upon himself. This almost repetitious statement insists on each one's grave personal responsibility in partaking of the Lord's Supper. What risks being overlooked in the statement itself is the use of *body* in the phrase "discerning the body." The term is used equivocally: it is the Body of Christ that comes together "when you assemble as a church" (11:18) to eat the Lord's Supper; and it is also "my body which is for you" (11:24) that they eat. You must "discern" in your fellow worshiper a member of the Body of Christ, that you may partake of the body of Christ.

By way of corollary, we must note the supreme appropriateness of "Body of Christ" to describe the church. The Body of Christ, of which more is said in the next chapter, is also the eucharistic body for us, so that we come together as the Body of Christ to celebrate the Eucharist, and, celebrating it, we in turn become the Body of Christ. Though Vatican II has retrieved a number of images of the church, the first and foremost is and remains the Body of Christ.

11:30 That is why many of you are weak and ill, and some have died. Paul, like Jesus and his disciples in the Gospels, is a child of his time, heir to an outlook that linked sickness and death with sin. The "fiery serpents" that bit the people of Israel in the desert and caused many of them to die were a punishment for the sin of rebellion against God (Num 21:5–7). Jesus, having healed the paralytic by the pool of Bethzatha, said to him, "See, you are well! Sin no more, that nothing worse befall you" (John 5:14; 8:11). The disciples ask Jesus about the man born blind, "Rabbi, who sinned, this man or his parents, that he was born blind?" (John 9:2). Paul is merely reminding the Corinthians of what they, too, believe: their sin against the Lord's Supper is punishable by illness and death. We no longer view the consequences of sin the same way; but we cannot for that reason deny the fact of sin in our lives nor the consequent need of divine forgiveness.

11:31 But if we judged ourselves truly, we should not be judged. This reminder merely reiterates the "Let a man examine himself, and so eat of the bread and drink of the cup" (11:28). It calls for the total lucidity about ourselves and the conduct that should mark all our days. The responsibility is squarely on each individual's shoulders. It cannot be shunted onto someone else, whatever her or his exalted status in the church. Alas, we have grown accustomed to evade the responsibility of judging ourselves "truly" by leaving it in someone else's hand: "Can I...?" "Is it okay if...?" "What if I...?" It can be a challenge for students in theological schools to explore their faith in order to provide in-depth answers to genuine questions rather than simply to prepare ready answers.

11:32 But when we are judged by the Lord, we are chastened so that we may not be condemned along with the world. Judging ourselves is in fact confessing our sins. Christianity is where our sins are always forgiven by the blood of Christ. This is an uninterrupted and never-ending process that goes on "until he comes" (11:26). It is simple in the extreme. Its most appropriate setting is, of course, the Supper of the Lord. Its neglect inevitably brings condemnation "along with the world;" for not even God can forgive an unrepentant sinner. The world, however, is ever averse to the exposure of its works as evil. It acknowledges no sin and recognizes no forgiveness. Therefore, it is "condemned."

11:33–34 So then, my brethren, when you come together to eat, wait for one another—... The closure of the instruction on the Lord's Supper comes back to its central issue. When you come together to eat, that is, to eat the Supper of the Lord, make sure you come together as the Body of Christ, aware and respectful of the other for whom Christ died (8:11). After all, you come together for one purpose and one purpose only: to "proclaim the Lord's death until he comes" (11:26).

146

if any one is hungry, let him eat at home—lest you come together to be condemned. The imperative of Christian life is so simple that the simplest can comprehend it without recourse to moral manuals or canonical pandects. Being simple, of course, does not mean it is easy. Hence the need for Paul to keep driving the point home. He is neither against the abundance of one's goods nor against their enjoyment: "Let him eat at home!" What he is adamantly against is humiliating those who have nothing (11:22). He never tires of putting the responsibility of the celebration of the Lord's Supper on each member of the Body of Christ.

About the other things I will give directions when I come.

Chapter 12

FIRST CORINTHIANS 12

12:1 Now concerning spiritual gifts, brethren, I do not want you to be uninformed. The "now concerning" phrase signals another question put to Paul in the letter from Corinth. For the Greek here, "spiritual gifts" is simply *pneumatika,* and can refer to spiritual gifts or spiritual persons. The subsequent discussion seems to have in view both the gifts and those who possess them. After all, a gift is not an abstraction. It is a gift if given by a giver and accepted by a recipient. There is, clearly, some misunderstanding about these *pneumatika* in Corinth, and Paul sets about to clarify the issue. Being "uninformed" could have woeful consequences in Corinth, even as it has had through the centuries in the church.

12:2 You know that when you were heathen, you were led astray to dumb idols, however you may have been moved. Paul prefaces his remarks by reminding the Corinthians of their former situation as "heathens"—"Gentiles" would be closer in meaning to the Greek *ethnē* here. Anyone slightly acquainted with the Greco-Roman literature of antiquity, even through works of fiction, has some general idea of how entangled the life of the individual was with the gods, temple sacrifices, votive offerings, magical powers, and dreams. It is, therefore, by no means surprising that once converted to the Christian faith they did not discard that mentality overnight, even if they ostensibly set aside their beliefs in the gods. They were much enamored of the spectacular and extraordinary manifestations of the Spirit (*pneuma*), and they aspired and actively sought such "spiritual" gifts (*pneumatika*) in the rich

atmosphere of the nascent church. The more dazzling and outlandish the gifts the more desirable they were.

The beginnings of religious movements are, more often than
not, accompanied by extraordinary and dazzling phenomena.
Christianity and the movements it spawned were no exception.
Doubtless, Corinth had its share of such manifestations of the
Spirit among its converts. So it is quite understandable that many
Christians aspired to the possession of such *pneumatika*. Naturally
enough, they envied one another's spiritual gifts, whether speaking in tongues, healing, working miracles, or what have you. The
mere possession of a different gift by another proved irresistible.

*12:3 Therefore I want you to understand that no one speaking by
the Spirit of God ever says "Jesus be cursed!" and no one can say
"Jesus is Lord" except by the Holy Spirit.* Paul does not question the
fact of the extraordinary gifts, the *pneumatika*; he merely lays
down the criteria for evaluating them. The first criterion he sets
down has been designated, for lack of a better term, the criterion
of orthodoxy. Anyone claiming to speak by the Spirit of God cannot possibly say, "Jesus is cursed!" (the Greek for "cursed" is
anathema). On the other hand, anyone saying, "Jesus is Lord,"
can only do so "by the Holy Spirit." In other words, an individual
with a patently false Christology cannot give expression to it by
the Holy Spirit, however impressive or brilliant she or he sounds.
Bad Christology cannot be attributable to the Holy Spirit.

This is a necessary reminder to any community alive with
manifestations of the Holy Spirit, particularly in its liturgical
assemblies. The criterion Paul sets for the Corinthians is not
meant to stifle the inspired individuals but to safeguard the faith
of the weaker members of the community. As good Christology
can only come from the inspiration of the Holy Spirit, so bad
Christology cannot possibly come from the same Spirit, whatever
the claim of the one who professes it. After all, Christology is
nothing but the statement of who Jesus is for the believer: the
Lord, the Christ, the Son of God, and so on. Each title constitutes

a Christology; and the assembly of the faithful gather together precisely to proclaim this Lordship "until he comes" (11:26).

Long after the cessation of the phenomena here referred to, the criterion of orthodoxy remains unaltered and inviolable. The solicitude of the Christian community in its entirety, and not just of its leaders, is to safeguard the integrity of its Christology, particularly as it is manifested in worshiping Jesus Christ as Lord.

12:4 Now there are varieties of gifts, but the same Spirit;... Paul's undoubted genius as a theologian comes through in instances like this. The Corinthians were enamored of spiritual gifts, the *pneumatika*, the more unusual the better. Like so many of our own contemporaries, "spiritual" held a siren charm for them. They tended to accentuate "spiritual" and chose not to stress "gift." By adroitly switching the accent to the fact that these were gifts (in the Greek, *charismata*, plural of *charisma*), he reminds the Corinthians of a few basic truths that they are only too apt to forget.

First of all, though there be a great variety of gifts, there is, and there can only be, one Spirit who is the source of all of them, from the most spectacular to the humblest. Insist on the superiority and excellence of one gift over the others, set the unusual and the outlandish at a premium, or give the impression that somehow you have cornered the market on the Spirit, and mark how discord and division fragment the community. The sure safeguard against such fragmentation is the reminder that all gifts in the community are from one and "the same Spirit."

12:5 and there are varieties of service, but the same Lord;... No gift (*charisma*) is ever conferred as an ornament on any individual in the community, from the most eminent to the least. Gift implies obligation. Every gift is given to be used in the service (Greek: *diakonia*) of that community. Each charism (*charisma*) is granted with a view to ministry (*diakonia*). Although the ministries themselves vary, and though service can take very many forms, it is always in obedience to the same Lord that they are exercised. As the Spirit is the source of unity in the varieties of charisms, so too the Lord is the source of authority in the service these charisms render the community.

12:6 and there are varieties of working [NRSV: activities], but it is the same God who inspires [NRSV: activates] them all in every one. That the variety of charisms and the multiplicity of ministries all work together in harmony for the good of the community can only be due, of course, to the one God who "inspires" or "activates" them all. Note the momentous shift of accent operated by Paul, from the solipsistic boast of individuals proud of their spiritual possessions (the *pneumatika*), to the stress on the nature of the gifts (*charismata*): the unity of their source, the same Spirit; the authority behind their exercise in the ministry, the same Lord; and the harmony of their achieved end, "the same God."

A word on the use of *Spirit*, *Lord*, and *God* in such close conjunction in these three verses (12:3, 4, and 5). Future generations will regard the verses as "trinitarian," and they will be right to do so if they keep in mind that it took three or four centuries before the church could speak properly about the Holy Trinity. But, until the time it became possible to do so, we should be content to speak of such formulae in the New Testament as "triadic" (see, for example, Rom 1:4; 2 Cor 13:14; Gal 4:6).

12:7 To each is given the manifestation of the Spirit for the common good. This is the second criterion for the use of the charisms in the community: all the "manifestations of the Spirit" have one purpose in sight: "the common good." Paul is content to repeat that the charisms (*charismata*), so dear to the heart of the Corinthians, are indeed manifestations of the Spirit (*pneumatika*). They are all ordained, not for the preening of the individual but for the good of the community. As we have had occasion to remark earlier, the gifts, the charisms, conferred on each believer are not an ornament but a burden. They are conferred on the individual only to be put at the service of the community of those who call on Jesus Christ as Lord.

12:8 To one is given through the Spirit the utterance of wisdom, and to another the utterance of knowledge according to the same Spirit,... Paul understands grace not as we commonly do, as a divine aid to a good deed. To him, grace is the individual's appropriation by faith of the Christ event, that is, the death and resurrection of Christ. When a believer believes that Christ died and rose from the dead "for me," that reality is what Paul understands by the gift of grace (Rom 3:24; Gal 1:6). But this grace is conferred on a unique individual with her or his personal characteristics, talents, abilities, limitations, and so on. Such individuation of grace is what Paul calls "charism." Evidently, then, each believer, without exception, possesses the charism peculiar to her or to him. All believers are, therefore, charismatic.

Thus, when one has the gift, the charism, to communicate wisdom to the congregation of believers, to bring before them a deeper understanding of the revelation of Christ Jesus with a view to their living it out more fully, such a person has the charism of wisdom. Another has the charism—no small one—of enlightening the minds of believers in the articles of their faith. To one as to the other, the source of the individual charism is always the one Spirit.

12:9 to another faith by the same Spirit, to another gifts of healing by the one Spirit,... The charism of "faith" in this context refers, in all likelihood, to the power of working miracles. Its juxtaposition with the "gifts of healing" makes such interpretation plausible. Yet the explicit mention of "the working of miracles" in the very next verse calls such interpretation into question. It is, therefore, best to admit one's ignorance on this point. What matters in this passage, however, is Paul's insistence that whatever the charism, it is always given by the Spirit and operates by the Spirit. The whole section is, of course, on spiritual gifts, that is, the charisms.

12:10 to another the working of miracles, to another prophecy, to another the ability to distinguish between spirits, to another various kinds of tongues, to another the interpretation of tongues. The ferment of enthusiasm in a nascent community yielded an abundance of charismatic gifts, some less familiar than others. Paul simply rounds off the listing of such gifts with a list that is, surely, not meant to be comprehensive. The important thing is that such charismatic gifts are conferred not on groups of people but on distinct individuals. Even when two possess the same charism, such as "prophecy" or the "ability to distinguish between spirits," each one of them will necessarily possess the gift in his or her own unique, inimitable fashion.

A brief word here is necessary about two of the charisms. Prophecy in the Old Testament consisted primarily in declaring the will of the Lord for his holy people, Israel: "Thus says the Lord!" It is only in the New Testament period that the term came to mean foretelling future events, principally because the New Covenant was understood as the fulfillment of Old Testament prophecy. In the present context, *prophecy* may well mean this foretelling of things to come, but it cannot exclude its original meaning of the courage to declare to God's people the Word of the Lord. More often than not, prophecy involves saying what no one wants to hear, speaking the unpalatable truth, reminding the people of what they would fain forget. This, indeed, is a gift of the Spirit.

The second charism that calls for comment is "the ability to distinguish between spirits." The "discernment of spirits," an accurate enough rendition of the Greek phrase in First Corinthians, is much in vogue at present, thanks perhaps to the conjunction of Ignatian–Jesuit spirituality and popular psychology. Whether such understanding of the phrase in Corinthians is legitimate remains moot. What Paul means by this very precious, and generally quite rare, charism is the ability to discern good from evil within the community and in the world, and the courage to call the evil by its name, wherever it be found. In this perspective, such a charism has much in common with the charism of prophecy in the Christian community. The proximity of one to the other in the listing may well be more than fortuitous.

12:11 All these are inspired [NRSV: activated] by one and the same Spirit, who apportions [NRSV: allots] to each one individually as he wills. The verse reiterates for the sake of emphasis the principal point that the Holy Spirit is at the source of all the charisms, the spiritual gifts. It is the one and the same Spirit who "allots" to each individual believer a particular, individual charism. It is the one and the same Spirit that "activates," renders effective, these charisms in the individuals who possess them. It is the Spirit who alone allots, assigns, apportions "to each one individually as he wills." Therefore, it is utterly vain, not to say impious, to arrogate to oneself the right to distribute and assign charisms in the church. Since the Spirit allots to each one individually as he wills, envy, emulation, comparisons, and jealousy among the believers of all ranks are exercises in utter futility.

12:12 For just as the body is one and has many members, and all the members of the body, though many, are one body, so it is with Christ. A truly great theologian embarks here on a theme that he already broached in 10:17 ("Because there is one bread, we who are many are one body, for we all partake of the one bread") and provides Christian theology with one of its most imposing themes: the Body of Christ. Paul sets forth a parallel, "just as...so," between the human body, which is constituted as a unity precisely by and through the multiplicity and diversity of its members, and the similarly constituted Body of Christ. Without this multiple diversity of the members there can be no one body. Without the unity of the diverse members there can be no body, but merely an agglomerate of disparate and disjointed parts.

"So it is with Christ." If this dazzling insight was not original with Paul—and there is no reason to doubt that it was—then he most certainly was the first to develop and exploit it. At his hands it became the means of expounding the meaning of the eucharistic body as well as of developing an ecclesiology of the ministerial charisms.

154

12:13 For by one Spirit we were all baptized into one body—Jews or Greeks, slaves or free—and all were made to drink of one Spirit. Ecclesiology begins with the sacrament of incorporation into the Body of Christ. Therefore, this body preexists its members. It is not and cannot be the result of their will, the outcome of a democratic vote, or of some social contract. The members do not bring about the existence of the body, but are incorporated into it, into an already existing entity. This is bound to come as a surprise to many contemporaries who are set on establishing a church to their own norms and specifications, a sociological structure erected by the preference and vote of its constitutive members.

The diversity of the members of the body is expressed by "Jews or Greeks, slave or free." The list is not exhaustive, of course, but all inclusive. What ought to be kept in mind, however, is that, in the Body of Christ, Jews do not lose their identity as Jews (see, for example, Paul writing to the Philippians: "circumcised on the eighth day, of the people of Israel, of the tribe of Benjamin, a Hebrew born of Hebrews"; Phil 3:5), nor do the Greeks. The slaves no more lose their status than the free. It is precisely this endless diversity that is "baptized into one body." It is their membership in the body that puts them all on equal footing at the Supper of the Lord.

The same Paul who at the start of his epistle reminded the Corinthians that "Christ did not send me to baptize but to preach the gospel" (1:17) here reminds the same Corinthians that baptism is the means of incorporation into the one Body of Christ. He thus provides the fundamental theological insight into the sacrament of baptism. Over the centuries, this insight was dissipated in the endless controversies on infant baptism and on the role of the sacrament in removing the stain of original sin. In the light of Paul's insight, we must keep in mind that the child of members of the Body of Christ has every right to belong to the same body. The parents bring the baby to the font because he or she is a member of their household, an integral part of their family.

Moreover, it is incorporation into the Body of Christ that cleanses us of all sins, not the other way around. Baptism incorporates us into the Body of Christ and, in so doing, makes us Christ's (3:23) and, therefore, holy, sanctified in Christ Jesus (1:2). Our holiness is the result of our belonging to the Body of Christ, not its condition.

The baptism that is at the source of our unity is "by one Spirit." This Spirit is, of course, the Spirit of Christ the Lord. It is what effects the unity of the body, for by it the many "were all baptized into one body," and—lest the eucharistic overtone be missed—Paul adds, "All were made to drink of one Spirit." The Letter to the Romans offers the apostle another opportunity to make explicit this insight:

> Do you not know that all of us who have been baptized into Christ Jesus were baptized into his death? We were buried therefore with him by baptism into death, so that as Christ was raised from the dead by the glory of the Father, we too might walk in newness of life. (Rom 6:3–4)

12:14 For the body does not consist of one member but of many. A reminder of the obvious is not always superfluous. In this context, such reminder is necessary because the attitude of the Corinthians betrays if not an ignorance of the obvious then at least blindness to its implications. It is not just that a body has many and different parts, but that without them it cannot be a body.

12:15–16 If the foot should say, "Because I am not a hand, I do not belong to the body," that would not make it any less a part of the body. And if the ear should say, "Because I am not an eye, I do not belong to the body," that would not make it any less a part of the body. The implication of these examples is obvious. In Corinth, as in today's church, it was and is all too common for the majority of the faithful to assume a supine attitude of indifference, leaving the workings of the community to those in high places. To them, church means the hierarchy. Of course, because of the smallness of the community in Corinth, such an attitude would not have been as sharply in evidence as it is in today's church.

12:17 If the whole body were an eye, where would be the hearing? If the whole body were an ear, where would be the sense of smell? There are proverbs and apologues aplenty in literature to illustrate the absurdity of this position. In Corinth, it was the rush to acquire the one or other of the prized spectacular charisms that another has and I haven't. In today's church, it is the equally absurd pretension that we all have the same charism, so that no hierarchy of gifts can be tolerated, and everyone is on the same democratic footing of equality. Everyone, with or without any qualification, is an expert theologian expatiating spurious opinions culled from the morning's paper.

12:18 But as it is, God arranged the organs in the body, each one of them, as he chose. This is another commonplace that the Corinthians, no less than we, tend to overlook. The Creator's role in who we are, the gifts and abilities each of us possesses, the functions we exercise, are all part of the first article of our Creed. It is so easy to forget that, in everything, this God "works for good with those who love him, who are called according to his purpose" (Rom 8:28).

12:19 If all were a single organ, where would the body be? This merely sums up the quasi self-evident truths formulated in the previous verses (12:14–18). A body cannot be a body without different parts, organs, members. Diversity and multiplicity make up the body, not tossed helter-skelter but arranged in a harmonious organic whole, ordained by God, "each one of them, as he chose" (12:18). Thus, the diversity and the multiplicity of the parts is essential to the organic unity of the body and to its ordered functioning.

12:20 As it is, there are many parts, yet one body. This might seem much like a reiterated platitude. Its insistence, however, is on the "one body." The unity of this one body, it must be kept in mind, is constituted precisely by the "many parts." What is in view here is definitely not the sterile uniformity of these parts, but their dynamic unity in diversity.

12:21 The eye cannot say to the hand, "I have no need of you," nor again the head to the feet, "I have no need of you." If such disdain of the lesser members was a painful phenomenon in a community as small as Corinth's, it is, alas, an institutionalized reality in today's church. To be sure, the "head" or the "eye" in today's church is not so crude as to put it as bluntly as Paul does. But this, in effect, is the reigning attitude: "You just do what you are told!" "Don't bother your head with theology!" "Say your prayers and leave such matters to us!" and so on, and so on. The very members who proudly vaunt their status and insist on their authority are quickest to remind the rest of the virtue of humility. It is a never ceasing wonder how, in the hands of the "superior" members, the gospel of freedom can become an instrument of tyranny and subjugation of the "hands," the "feet," and the "unpresentable parts" without which the body cannot exist.

12:22 On the contrary, the parts of the body which seem to be weaker are indispensable,... The church is, to be sure, a hierarchy, but it is a hierarchy stood on its head. This verse opens a sustained argument that insists precisely on this point. What society can you think of in which the weaker members are "indispensable"? Such a point of view can only be urged in a community of those who follow a Lord who humbled himself, "taking the form of a servant" (Phil 2:7–8).

12:23–24 and those parts of the body which we think less honorable we invest with the greater honor, and our unpresentable parts are treated with greater modesty, which our more presentable parts do not require. This can strike many of our contemporaries as naive in the extreme. But, in civilized societies, in the East at least if not in the West, this sentiment is taken for granted. Pudicity, personal modesty, is integral to human dignity. Whatever the personal opinion on the metaphor Paul employs here, the essential point he makes is beyond cavil. In the community of believers, the insignificant, the despised, those whose presence in the assembly causes averted gazes and embarrassed discomfort, are those who require the "greater honor" and care and respect. That such a point of view strikes some as unusual or outlandish is no argument against its veracity.

But God has so composed the body, giving the greater honor to the inferior part,... The composition of the body is a divinely ordained reality. In the Body of Christ, greater honor is due the inferior parts. This is indeed an upside-down hierarchical order, but it is, nevertheless, an order willed by God. The inexhaustible riches of the community as the Body of Christ are ever more plainly displayed in these chapters (1 Cor 12–14). It is incomprehensible how neglected they are. In them, the inferiors are accorded superior attention, the negligible matter greatly, and the disgraceful are shown respect. One can only wonder what those who today are intent on dismantling and reorganizing the members of the Body of Christ do have in mind for the "democratic" church they wish to substitute for it. There is more than one way to void Paul's message of its force.

12:25 that there may be no discord in the body, but that the members may have the same care for one another. This is the twofold aim toward which the argument for a topsy-turvy hierarchical church has tended. The twofold aim embraces the harmony of the body, that is, the absence of discord among its members and the care they must have for one another. In fact, the twofold aims are one: taking care of one another eliminates discord and fosters harmony in the Body of Christ. The argument at times may seem rotatory, but it is steadily progressing toward its inevitable climax.

12:26 If one member suffers, all suffer together; if one member is honored, all rejoice together. This only makes explicit what having the same care for one another is. "To suffer together" is but a par-

159

aphrase of "sympathy." It marks the true attitude of the Christian to all the less fortunate. Such an attitude is by no means exclusive to Christians. But, for those who follow a crucified redeemer, it is the peculiar cachet that marks their membership in the Body of Christ.

If sympathy with those who suffer seems relatively easy, almost spontaneous, at times, rejoicing with a member who is honored requires a wholly particular exertion. Indeed, loving the other is evident in sharing the beloved's suffering. The real, the arduous, test is genuine joy at the success, good fortune, achievement of the other. Rejoicing together is nothing less than the hallmark of authentic love, of true care for one another.

12:27 Now you are the body of Christ and individually members of it. This is the climax toward which the previous argument has tended from the start. It is a simple statement of identity: "You *are* the body of Christ." Paul does not say, "You are like the body of Christ," but simply, "You are!" without further qualification. A moment's reflection should suffice to reveal how all the preceding remarks and instructions in the epistle are grounded on this one incontrovertible theological indicative. The questions on various factions, on party spirit, on sexual immorality, on litigation, on marital problems, on food offered to idols, on the gifts and charisms of the Spirit, and so on, all find their resolution in this "You are the body of Christ."

To add "and individually members of it" makes explicit what is already in the fundamental statement. The multiplicity and diversity of the members is constitutive of the unity of the body. No understanding of the body is possible without the realization that each and every one of its members is individually a member of the Body of Christ and, consequently, of infinite worth and value in the community that calls upon his name.

12:28–30 And God has appointed in the church first apostles, second prophets, third teachers, then workers of miracles, then healers, helpers, administrators, speakers in various kinds of tongues. Are all apostles? Are all prophets? Are all teachers? Do all work miracles? Do all possess gifts of healing? Do all speak with tongues? Do all interpret? The hierarchical order, logical though it be, is ordained by God. Paul here simply delineates a diversity of charisms in their order of precedence. The essential is not who is first and who is second, but that an orderly hierarchy is maintained among them. One might be disposed today to accept the "first apostles" and yet would still be hard put to determine where, in today's church, one can fit "workers of miracles [NRSV has "deeds of power," whatever these may be]" or "healers" [NRSV: "gifts of healing"]. In other words, the list reflects the community as Paul knew it. It is not meant to be valid in perpetuity.

A generation after Paul's, the author of the Letter to the Ephesians limits himself to naming only the first three charisms but sets the hierarchic order in a profoundly purposive context:

> And his gifts were that some should be apostles, some
> prophets, some evangelists, some pastors and teachers,
> to equip the saints for the work of ministry, for building
> up the body of Christ, until we all attain to the unity of
> the faith and of the knowledge of the Son of God, to
> mature manhood, to the measure of the stature of the
> fullness of Christ. (Eph 4:11–13)

A word on the word "administrators" [the NRSV, less felicitously, has "leaders"] in Paul's list is called for here, because the general tendency in today's church is to assign this category the first rank in the hierarchical order. The Greek word employed is *kybernēseis*, meaning helmsman, steersman, the pilot who guides the vessel into port (whence we have the modern "cybernetics"). It is not the intention here to dispute where the charism of administrator fits in today's hierarchy, but merely to call attention that governance is indeed a charism and, therefore, piloting the ship into a safe haven, steering it clear of the shoals and shallows, is subject to all the criteria that determine the use of any other charism. Administrators, in other words, are not an exempt category apart.

What Paul stresses in this passage is that not every member can fulfill the identically same function in the body. The diversity of functions is essential for the life of the body. Not all can be prophets, nor all can be teachers, nor all apostles, desirable and prestigious though such charisms be. Like all charisms, these are not concentrated in one person, nor can any member possess them cumulatively. Their very diversity is constitutive of the body. Each one of them, the highest as well as the lowest among them, is essential for equipping the "saints for the work of ministry, for building up the body of Christ" (Eph 4:12).

12:31 But earnestly desire the higher gifts. And I will show you a still more excellent way. The Corinthians were agog with the desire for spectacular gifts, the *pneumatika*. Paul directs their gaze to the "higher gifts" (*charismata*), even if they may not seem to redound to the self-esteem of their possessor. They are intended, and in fact are meant, for the greater service of the entire body, not for the self-aggrandizement of any individual.

The chapter (1 Cor 12) opened with "concerning spiritual gifts," *pneumatika*, those extraordinary manifestations of the Spirit that so bewitched the Corinthians, and even today do not lack fascination for many in the church. Paul, as was noted previously (see on 12:4), with great theological incisiveness, redirects the attention to the "gift" nature, the charismatic quality, of all the manifestations of the Spirit in the community. The same chapter now concludes precisely by speaking not of spiritual gifts (*pneumatika*) but of charisms, the *charismata*. In so doing, he forms another rhetorical *inclusio* that binds the chapter together.

The transition to the next chapter, the center of the three on charisms (1 Cor 12, 13, and 14) calls for special comment because it has occasioned a perennial misunderstanding. Having just exhorted the Corinthians to "earnestly desire the higher gifts" (*charismata*), he abruptly adds, "And I will show a still more excellent way." He does not say "a more excellent charism," for the simple reason that love, the subject of the next chapter, is not a charism, but that by which charisms are what they are. It is not enough for the believer to possess this or that gift. An individual's gift can be called a charism only, and only as long as the gift is put at the service of the other, that is, exercised in love. What makes a gift a charism is precisely the love that impels its possessor to use it in the service of the other.

Chapter 13

FIRST CORINTHIANS 13

13:1–3 If I speak in the tongues of men and of angels, but have not love, I am a noisy gong or a clanging cymbal. And if I have prophetic powers, and understand all mysteries and all knowledge, and if I have all faith, so as to remove mountains, but have not love, I am nothing. If I give away all I have, and if I deliver my body to be burned, but have not love, I gain nothing. The reiterated "if" statements are, of course, a rhetorical device, quite common in Paul's day, and a perennial plague of politicians in our own. The marked difference between the two usages, past and present, lies in Paul's ability to harness the device to establish a rational argument.

As already noted, although love itself is not a charism, it is that without which no charism can exist. Hence, the all-embracing list of those spiritual gifts, the *pneumatika*, that the Corinthians found most prestigious and, therefore, most attractive, is conveniently summed up in these verses (13:1–3). The list begins, understandably enough, with that spectacular gift of speaking in tongues. Without love, this gift, no matter how extraordinary in its manifestation, is no more than noise, the reboant clangor of a vacuum, what Augustine called a "voice" (*vox*) without the "word" (*verbum*), mere noise. For speaking in tongues to be a genuine charism, it must be exercised in love, out of love for the other and not for oneself.

Similarly, high on the list of desiderata among the spiritual gifts is the trio of prophecy, "the utterance of wisdom…and knowledge" (12:8), and faith (12:9). Whoever possesses these but has not love is utterly "nothing." It is as though, without love, the person, however richly endowed, has no existence.

The climax of the series is almost hyperbolic. It is that because of the difficulty of conceiving anyone giving away his possessions and delivering himself up to be burned without love. Yet, Paul insists, as it were *per impossibile*, should anyone do such a thing without love, then the deed itself, however admirable and praiseworthy, would be utterly futile. It would be as though it never took place.

Love, therefore, is the absolute, indispensable condition for the exercise of any and all of the charisms, from the greatest to the least, from the most extraordinary to the humblest.

13:4–6 Love is patient and kind; love is not jealous or boastful; it is not arrogant or rude. Love does not insist on its own way; it is not irritable or resentful; it does not rejoice at wrong, but rejoices in the right. To obviate any need for questions about his meaning, Paul goes on not to define love but to describe it. He does this, first, by naming two of its qualities: "Love is patient and kind." Love, in fact, is one precisely because it is the other. It is patient in waiting upon the other, allowing her or him that precious commodity, time; and this is quintessential kindness. Love is kind in avoiding giving the impression that it has more important things to attend to. It possesses the magnanimity of allowing the other to enjoy the leisurely infinitude of the present moment.

Paul follows the two positive qualities of love with a series of mostly negative ones. Nothing can occasion arrogance and rudeness like the exercise of one's gifts. The loftier the gift and the humbler its object, the more impatient becomes its exercise. Impatience here begets rudeness and arrogance. Genuine love makes the exercise of any charism seem effortless and almost imperceptible: "The greater the love, the less the labor," reminds us Saint Augustine. It is generally true that only those most destitute of any genuine charism, not because they are not "gifted" but because they lack love, are the rudest and most arrogant of their kind. They rant pious platitudes and bluster empty anathemas to hide their emptiness and destitution. The higher the position they occupy and the greater the authority they wield, the more evident their lack of love becomes.

If love "does not insist on its own way," it is simply because it is the nature of love to go out of itself to the other. Genuine love leaves the other wholly free to be where and as he or she is. Duns Scotus remarked that "to say I love you is to say that I wish you to be as you are." Such love does not try to refashion the other in its own image and likeness. In the final analysis, those who try to do so love only themselves. Moreover, insistence on its own way is what makes love "irritable or resentful." The object of your ministration remains always free to reject what you judge to be your irresistible reasoning, or winning charm, or compelling theological truth.

Rejoicing at the wrong is one aspect of loveless arrogance. Nowadays, it comes garbed in the devious refusal to call evil by its name, the demurral to be judgmental. Recognizing evil for what it is finds its reverse in rejoicing in the right, which is the true mark of loving membership in the body: "If one member suffers, all suffer together; if one member is honored, all rejoice together" (1 Cor 12:26). Herein lies the true test of love: the ability to rejoice in the beloved's good fortune.

There were in Corinth, as in today's church, those who take particular delight in discoursing volubly on the ills and evils of the church. The more nefarious the deeds they uncover, the more gleeful they are in their exposition. It is never easy for such people to remember that if the church is indeed a church of sinners, it is because they themselves, like you and me, belong to it. They ought to keep in mind, as should also their long-suffering audience, that the only valid criticism of the church can come from those who truly love the Body of Christ and its members. Without this love, the rejoicing in evil, the spate of invectives, is bound to be in the end no more than "a noisy gong or a clanging cymbal." Criticism from outside the fold is ineffective and sterile. In the end, only the loving criticism of the living member can give life.

13:7 Love bears all things, believes all things, hopes all things, endures all things. Love is necessarily long suffering as long as it is in this mutable and transient world. If love is patient with its object, then long-suffering befits its subject. The lover must ever be on her or his guard against the tendency to be "irritable or resentful" (13:5).

Similarly, the one who loves must shun skepticism in all its myriad forms. This is the meaning of love "believes all things." It cannot indulge the compulsion to question and examine the one whom it loves. It must be willing to believe the other as and where she or he is. Nothing can be more deleterious to an encounter than that hint of affected cynicism to which the modern world has accustomed us. If love is willing to accept the other as and where the other is, then hope must mark its progress from first loving the other to better knowledge of the other, to still greater love as a consequence of this new knowledge, *et sic ad infinitum*; that is, there is and there can be no end to this progression, as 13:13 clearly affirms.

Because love of the other is expressed in this mutable world of mortality and all its attendant vicissitudes, it requires endurance, the quality that hoops together patience, longsuffering, and hope.

13:8 Love never ends; as for prophecies, they will pass away; as for tongues, they will cease; as for knowledge, it will pass away. In a passing world, where decay and death are the rule, it is only love that abides, only love that knows no end: "Love is not love / Which alters when it alteration finds." All the charisms to which the Corinthians aspired are doomed to cease. Their utility is contingent upon existence in this world. Love, genuine love, is of the fabric of eternity. When I love the other, there is, there can be, no end to it. Christianity knows no one-night stands.

This quality of love is one clue to our understanding what we mean by the resurrection, as 1 Corinthians 15 provides us with the opportunity to see.

13:9–10 For our knowledge is imperfect and our prophecy is imperfect; but when the perfect comes, the imperfect will pass away. The

167

conditional nature of all the charisms betrays their imperfection. This is all the more necessary to keep in mind especially in those spiritual gifts that occupy such high ranks in the Christian community. Strange, indeed, how in the teeth of the evidence, those who possess knowledge of divine things and those who prophesy in the community, labor under the illusion of immortality, if not of themselves, then at least of their ideas. Their epigones pretend to sustain such illusion for a generation or two, but they and the object of their propaganda are doomed to "pass away."

The perfect comes only when love has the last word. When it does come, its very clarity casts all else into the shadow: prophecy, wisdom, knowledge, speaking in tongues, all cease to matter. As the poet put it, "What will survive of us is love."

13:11 When I was a child, I spoke like a child, I thought like a child, I reasoned like a child; when I became a man, I gave up childish ways. The progression from the immaturity of childhood to the maturity of manhood is a law of our existence in this changing world. Paul is intent upon reminding the Corinthians, indeed Christians of every generation, of their progress to the stature of maturity in Christ. Faith in Christ is not an invitation to infantile fixation on childhood's fancies.

Some years after Paul wrote First Corinthians, one of his followers penned a perfect description of what he says:

And his gifts were that some should be apostles, some prophets, some evangelists, some pastors and teachers, to equip the saints for the work of ministry, for building up the body of Christ, until we all attain to the unity of the faith and of the knowledge of the Son of God, to mature manhood, to the measure of the stature of the fulness of Christ; so that we may no longer be children, tossed to and fro and carried about with every wind of doctrine, by the cunning of men, by their craftiness in deceitful wiles. Rather, speaking the truth in love, we are to grow up in every way into him who is the head, into Christ, from whom the whole body, joined and knit together by every joint with which it is supplied, when each part is working properly, makes bodily growth and upbuilds itself in love. (Eph 4:11–16)

13:12 For now we see in a mirror dimly, but then face to face. Now I know in part; then I shall understand fully, even as I have been fully understood. A constant refrain throughout First Corinthians is the eschatological perspective that governs all Paul's arguments. This verse is no exception. To be sure, if our vision on this earth is partial, hereafter it will be "face to face." The expression is commonly but erroneously taken to mean an exhaustive knowledge of the other. No knowledge of the other can be exhaustive. If it were, then the knower and the known would be one and the same. The other remains forever the other. This is why Simone Weil could say that love is "consent to the fact that there is authentic otherness." However perfectly I know the other, there will forever be that which eludes my grasp and, consequently, calls for more love, which grows in knowledge that, in its turn, calls for still more love. This, by the way, is what constitutes the never-ceasing dynamic of eternity. Eternity can never be the popularly held passive contemplation of the all, a nonexercise that is bound to end in boredom even in the heavenly places.

The "even as I have been fully understood" is not some sort of mystical reciprocity of knowledge between the Creator and the creature. It is rather the expression of election by God: "But if one loves God, one is known by him" (8:3); "The Lord knows those who are his" (2 Tim 2:19; see Ps 139:1–12). Those, then, who attain to life in God's presence "will understand fully," a fullness that is inexhaustible, not just because its object is God but because its object is the unique other.

13:13 So faith, hope, love abide, these three; but the greatest of these is love. This is another statement that has had the misfortune of generating endless popularity and consequent misunderstanding. Popular piety, spiritual instruction, and even theological tracts seem never to tire of repeating that once we see God face to face, faith will be redundant and, should anyone inquire, so too will hope. This is most assuredly not what Paul says. He insists that the triad of faith, hope, and love, "these three," abides. All three abide simply because there can be no true love without both faith and hope. Where there is love, there of necessity must faith and hope also be, one because love is a relationship to the other, and the other because such relationship cannot subsist without a future. For this reason, Paul adds, "The greatest of these is love."

Though it is conceivable that there can be some form of faith without love, and though it is also conceivable that some kind of hope can exist without love, it is utterly inconceivable for love to exist without the one and the other. To quote again Simone Weil, who wrote so well about love and led so seemingly loveless an existence, "Faith is the experience that the intelligence is enlightened by love." This is true whenever you love the other, the unknown other, and try to understand her or him with an understanding that must hope to grow. Thus, love has to exercise faith in the other forever, seeking to understand the other, and hoping thereby to grow in knowledge and consequently in love of the other. Thus, though all three are destined to abide, it is love that is the greatest among them.

First Corinthians 13 comes in the middle of the discussion of the charisms. Its position is by no means fortuitous. Paul sets it there because it is love that makes the gifts of the Spirit real charisms. The rules that govern love ultimately govern all the charisms that the diverse members employ in ministering to God's holy people, in building up the Body of Christ. Perhaps this is why a commentator once remarked that, far from being a "hymn to love," as it is commonly called, First Corinthians 13 is a Christology. It describes the love with which Christ loves his Body, so that, as Saint Augustine said long ago, "There will ultimately be one Christ loving himself."

170

Chapter 14

FIRST CORINTHIANS 14

14:1 Make love your aim, and earnestly desire the spiritual gifts, especially that you may prophesy. The imperative of love must determine the entire life of the believer. It sums up what has been said about love in the previous chapter and gives all the spiritual gifts, the *pneumatika*, their reason for existing. Note how Paul, having insisted on the gift character of all these spiritual endowments as *charismata*, and having reminded the Corinthians that all the believers are charismatics, each possessing gifts of the Spirit, now goes on to describe their use in and for the community.

If the Corinthians seek after certain spiritual gifts in preference to others, Paul urges them to "strive...that you may prophesy" [NRSV]. This charism of prophecy was one especially needed in Corinth and—one can add without fear of demur—in today's church. Why should Paul single out this one charism as one to be striven for? Because, of all the charisms, it is the one least likely to win friends for the prophet. The community is rarely disposed to hear unpalatable truths or to be reminded of forgotten or abandoned imperatives; and this is the chief task of the prophet in its midst.

It is unnecessary to add that to prophesy here does not refer to foretelling the future. The triple function assigned to prophecy in 14:3 ought to make this clear. This prophesying is, as Paul will say, "for upbuilding and encouragement and consolation" of the believers, not to provide them with "estimated times of arrival" of this or the other event.

14:2 For one who speaks in a tongue speaks not to men but to God; for no one understands him, but he utters mysteries in the Spirit. Let me at the outset confess that I do not know what speaking in a tongue or in tongues means. Let me add that I have the temerity to assert that neither did Paul (14:18). Whatever the phenomenon intended, those present did not comprehend what was being said: "for no one understands him." It is only Paul's magnanimity, and perhaps also that of those who witnessed the phenomenon, to believe that whatever the speaker uttered was "mysteries in the Spirit." If what the speaker in tongues sounded was unintelligible, then how can anyone conclude to the substance of what he or she said? It is clear, however, that the purpose of the statement here is to set the stage for the contrast to what follows in the next verse.

14:3 On the other hand, he who prophesies speaks to men for their upbuilding and encouragement and consolation. In clear contrast to the charism of tongues, prophesying amply meets the second criterion of the charisms, the common good (12:7). In fact, this already adumbrates the soon to be formulated third criterion of the charisms: the building up of the church (14:5). A gift is a charism, a true gift of the Spirit, when it "builds up, encourages, and consoles" the community of believers in Jesus Christ. This triple function of prophecy in the community should obviate the need to explain why "that you may prophesy" in 14:1 is not, and cannot be, a reference to foretelling the future. It has to do with the good of the community here and now.

14:4 He who speaks in a tongue edifies himself, but he who prophesies edifies the church. Moreover, it is difficult to see how speaking in tongues can really "edify the church." Whatever benefit accrues to the person gifted with tongues, it is not easy to say what profit the other members of the community can derive from it, nor how the phenomenon itself can build up, encourage, or console anyone in the community besides the speaker.

Even the statement that he "edifies himself" must be taken on faith. If the speaker in a tongue says he has been edified, his statement, by its very nature, is non-falsifiable. However, "he who prophesies" builds up, edifies the church; and this certainly is verifiable. Thus, the charism of prophecy does contribute to the common good and is not just a parure disported by its possessor as some special mark of divine favor denied to lesser and less gifted members in the community.

14:5 Now I want you all to speak in tongues, but even more to prophesy. He who prophesies is greater than he who speaks in tongues, unless some one interprets, so that the church may be edified. Clearly, Paul does not "want you all to speak in tongues" any more than he wants all to prophesy. This is mere hyperbole. He who sets such high value on all things being done "decently and in order" (14:40), who limits the number of those prophesying to "two or three" (14:29), and who enjoins silence on all the rest is not very likely to encourage such brouhaha in the community. Paul, after all, is a child of the tradition that believes the Lord cannot be found in "the wind...the earthquake...the fire" but in a "small still voice" (1 Kgs 19:11–12). His God is "not a God of confusion" (1 Cor 14:33).

The Corinthians, who evidently prized speaking in tongues above all other gifts of the Spirit, needed a reminder that the one who prophesies is, beyond all doubt, "greater." But, in his attempt to be evenhanded, Paul adds, "unless some one interprets" what the speaker in tongues utters. If, however, "no one understands him" (14:2) in the first place, then where do you find an interpreter? Paul must surely realize that "unless some one interprets" is contrafactual. The argument, therefore, is simply *per impossibile*, that is, of the "when pigs fly" variety.

The concluding "so that the church may be edified" formulates the third criterion of the charisms: the criterion of faith, the so-called of orthodoxy (12:3); the criterion of the common good (12:7); and this, the edification, the building up, of the church. So, whatever gift a believer may possess, and however important and necessary it happens to be, it can only be a genuine spiritual gift, a charism, if it is exercised out of love, for the good of the others, and for the building up of the Body of Christ. Put bluntly, you employ your talents and gifts not to show off or to enhance your position in the community, but solely out of love for others, for their good, and for the good of the community at large. The gifts are not there to foster what, long before Nietzsche, Saint Augustine called the *libido dominandi*, the will to power. In other words, you put the gift to use in ministering to the community, not in lording it over them. All charisms are for service.

14:6 Now, brethren, if I come to you speaking in tongues, how shall I benefit you unless I bring you some revelation or knowledge or prophecy or teaching? The point at issue is intelligibility. Whatever is addressed to the believers must, of necessity, be comprehensible. It must make some sense, else it is just "a noisy gong or a clanging cymbal" (13:1).

14:7 If even lifeless instruments, such as the flute or the harp, do not give distinct notes, how will any one know what is played? And if the bugle gives an indistinct sound, who will get ready for battle? If the contention of those who speak in tongues is that they are lifeless, inert, or unconscious instruments of spiritual powers over which they themselves have no control, the intelligibility of their utterance is still the indispensable condition of its usefulness to the community. Neither gibberish nor cacophony can ever be a mark of divine revelation. This, by the way, is no less true of those who bewilder the minds of believers with impenetrable jargon in proclaiming the Christian message or in explaining its content to the members of the Body of Christ. Clarity of thought and lucidity of expression are the only acceptable coin of the realm in communicating "revelation or knowledge or prophecy or teaching" (14:6) to the church.

14:9–11 So with yourselves; if you in a tongue utter speech that is not intelligible, how will any one know what is said? For you will be speaking into the air. There are doubtless many different languages in the world, and none is without meaning; but if I do not know the mean-

174

ing of the language, I shall be a foreigner [Greek: barbaros] to the speaker and the speaker a foreigner [Greek: barbaros] to me. It would surely be difficult to put Paul's meaning more clearly. Such a straightforward statement of what he wishes to say to the Corinthians, without tergiversation and without periphrastic circumlocution, to which so much Christian discourse has accustomed us, ought to have set a pattern for the generations that followed him. Paul is careful to communicate his thought clearly and intelligibly, not because he is a saint or an apostle or an inspired author, but simply because he loves the Body of Christ and genuinely seeks to serve every single one of its members, even the very least.

14:12 So with yourselves; since you are eager for manifestations of the Spirit, strive to excel in building up the church. Nowhere is the Spirit more palpably present in the community than when the gospel is being proclaimed in its midst. But it is not enough to possess the charism of teaching, or preaching, or prophecy. Its possessor must forever strive to excel in its use, in order that the third criterion of the charisms, the "building up the church," be fulfilled. Every charismatic, that is to say every believer, is bound to work diligently at excelling in whatever charism she or he possesses. It is not enough to possess a charism. One must strive continually to excel in putting it at the service of the Body of Christ, not for self-aggrandizement, but for the building up of the church. Every true charismatic knows only too well what it means to say, "The love of Christ urges us" (2 Cor 5:14).

14:13 Therefore, he who speaks in a tongue should pray for the power to interpret. Intelligibility is stressed in exercising the charism of tongues. Paul takes for granted the genuineness of the experience and consequently exhorts the person to "pray for the power to interpret," the presumption being that the speaker must have some understanding of what she or he utters "in a tongue."

14:14–15 For if I pray in a tongue, my spirit prays but my mind is unfruitful. What am I to do? I will pray with the spirit and I will pray with the mind also; I will sing with the spirit and I will sing with the mind also. Clarity is not what one finds in these two verses. Its absence is some indication of how imperfectly Paul understood the phenomenon of tongues. The dichotomy of spirit and mind is not very helpful in this context. What one can gather is that praying in a tongue is not what one would call a rational activity, not when it leaves the mind "unfruitful." The solution suggested by Paul has every mark of improvisation: When in doubt, do both, pray and sing "with the spirit…and with the mind also," which does not advance the argument one bit. Being an apostle, any more than being ordained to the ministry, is not a guarantee of omniscience.

14:16 Otherwise, if you bless with the spirit, how can any one in the position of an outsider say the "Amen" to your thanksgiving when he does not know what you are saying? Paul's primary concern is the others in the assembly, those who do not possess this particular charism of tongues. For them, to participate intelligently in your prayers of thanksgiving (the Greek here is *eucharistia*, used in its first imposition of "giving thanks"), they need to understand what you are saying. Strangely enough, the church in the West read this text and went on for centuries blithely praying in a language utterly incomprehensible to the millions who responded "Amen" to what they did not understand.

14:17 For you may give thanks well enough, but the other man is not edified. We are back, once again, to the criterion of the charisms: edification, the building up of the community. A gift, however spectacular, is not a charism unless it be used to build up the Body of Christ. If it is not of service to the "other man," then it is simply not a charism, merely a talent that is the boast of its possessor. The believers are charismatics only if they put their gifts at the service of the other, for the upbuilding of the church.

By the way, in this connection it should be noted that the exercise of each charism carries with it the requisite authority. But what authority the possessor of a charism has in and for the duration of its exercise terminates with the conclusion of the exercise, be it prophecy, teaching, exhortation, instruction, or bell ringing. It does not carry into the marketplace. Ordination grants no one the ability to pronounce on any and every subject, in or out of the pulpit, all the year round.

14:18 I thank God that I speak in tongues more than you all;… In reality, Paul does not. This is no more than a rhetorical *boutade* of the "Whatever you can do I can do better" variety.

14:19 nevertheless, in church I would rather speak five words with my mind, in order to instruct others, than ten thousand words in a tongue. Are we to understand that Paul spoke in a tongue in his own domicile? In the privacy of his seclusion? To what end? No! The point he makes here is once again the need to put the charism at the service of others. Small, humble charisms at the service of the neighbor and the community, such as instructing the ignorant, far outweigh any brilliant display of "ten thousand words in a tongue."

14:20 Brethren, do not be children in your thinking; be babes in evil, but in thinking be mature. This much-needed reminder to Christian believers of every generation pertains to every age. Children's thinking is marked by gullibility, but a vast number of adults share this trait. It is easy enough to acquire and still easier to maintain. All it requires for thriving is a refusal to think, to subject what is handed to us to critical judgment. The exercise of critical judgment is the mark of the mature. They are not readily swayed hither and yon by the orotund affirmations of the pundits, be they in the ecclesiastical or the secular sphere. God provided all the "mature" with a mind, and they should never hesitate to use it, whatever the cost. There has never been room for "You say your prayers, and leave these matters to us."

14:21 In the law it is written, "By men of strange tongues and by the lips of foreigners will I speak to this people, and even then they

177

will not listen to me, says the Lord." A new argument on the phenomenon of tongues has occurred to Paul as he, in all likelihood, dictates this letter. He has recourse to the Scriptures that, to him as to Jesus, always meant the Old Testament. It is referred to here simply as "the law," even though the text cited is from the prophet Isaiah (28:11–12). Here again Paul cites the Greek version, the Septuagint (LXX).

One may rightly wonder whether Paul's repeated insistence on the phenomenon of tongues was not in fact falling on deaf ears. The text he cites from Isaiah was, in all likelihood, more for consoling himself than for swaying the Corinthian charismatic speakers in tongues.

14:22 Thus, tongues are a sign not for believers but for unbelievers, while prophecy is not for unbelievers but for believers. This seems hardly in need of saying, except for the puzzle of how tongues are a sign for unbelievers. Does Paul mean that unbelievers will inevitably be attracted and intrigued by this phenomenon? Unbelievers must surely have had equally fascinating phenomena in their temples, shrines, or marketplaces. The Corinthians could not have been very different from the Athenians, who "spent their time in nothing except telling or hearing something new" (Acts 17:21). Speaking in tongues must have possessed the fascination of novelty for them.

At the same time, that prophecy is meant for believers needs hardly be stated. The very presupposition is that prophecy enlightens the eyes of believers to the implications of their faith and calls them to respond courageously to its demands.

14:23 If, therefore, the whole church assembles and all speak in tongues, and outsiders or unbelievers enter, will they not say that you are mad? The response to this rhetorical question is obvious. But what might escape attention is that the church always has an obligation not to cause scandal to outsiders and nonbelievers. Its actions as a whole and the comportment of its members individually do matter a great deal. As the task of proclaiming the gospel is not confined to uttered words but must be manifest in deeds as well, so too its proclamation is extended to all the members of the church in their daily lives, even to those members who never have the occasion to utter a single word.

14:24 *But if all prophesy, and an unbeliever or outsider enters, he is convicted [NRSV: reproved] by all, he is called to account by all,...* The contrast here is between the cacophonous effect of tongues on unbelievers and outsiders and the compelling exhortation of prophecy on them. The Corinthians, like so many other Christian communities then and now, must have known those who, almost by accident, sometimes drift into a church at prayer, are somehow or other moved by the experience, and end up baptized into the Body of Christ. Such occurrence is the more readily credible if you reflect that it is by no means confined to the Christian religion.

14:25 *the secrets of his heart are disclosed; and so, falling on his face, he will worship God and declare that God is really among you.* Were it not for this verse, the meaning of "convicted" and "called to account" in the preceding verse would remain almost impenetrable. As it is, one might well suspect that the use of these terms is a catachresis, the wrong use of a word. Paul, like any other inspired or uninspired author, is quite susceptible to such misuse of the term. Inspiration does not alter the nature of the person inspired, nor does it improve the writer's grammar, syntax, or vocabulary. The Spirit does not do violence to the instrument of its divine action.

What the present verse (14:25) describes is a conversion. The outsider or unbeliever who drifts into the assembly is moved to compunction, confesses his sins, and turns to God from idols "to serve a living and true God" (1 Thess 1:9). Such an event is by no means as rare as some suppose.

14:26 *What then, brethren? When you come together, each one has a hymn, a lesson, a revelation, a tongue, or an interpretation. Let all things be done for edification.* "Edification" here is in its primary sense of building up. The Christian assembly is made up of a multiplicity of diverse charisms. The one thing that dictates their use and marks them as genuine charisms is edification, their exercise with a view to building up the church, to edifying the Body of Christ. If this end is within the purview of all those who put their charismatic gifts at the service of the community, then the instruction that follows is no more than common sense.

14:27 If any speak in a tongue, let there be only two or at most three, and each in turn; and let one interpret. The limit put on the number and the specification that each one speak in turn imply that the other one or two keep silence. As has thus far been made amply clear, speaking in a tongue is useless unless there is someone to interpret. One would have thought the exhortation unnecessary if every speaker in a tongue had the good of the community at heart. Evidently, they did not, and Paul had to remind them of the obvious:

14:28 But if there is no one to interpret, let each of them keep silence in church and speak to himself and to God. Possessing a gift gives you no unqualified right to exercise it. The gift of speaking in tongues necessarily requires an interpreter. If one cannot be found in the assembly, then the possessor of the gift should simply "keep silence." Unintelligible sound can be of no use save perhaps to its possessor, who can indulge the gift in private without imposing it on the worshiping community.

14:29 Let two or three prophets speak, and let the others weigh what is said. Even in the case of a charism whose utility is beyond dispute, Paul is careful to limit its exercise to "two or three." If the audience is to weigh what is said, to ponder its meaning, then each of the prophets must speak by turn, not all at once. So the other one or two prophets must the while keep silent and themselves listen. This, when all is said and done, is no more than ordinary civility.

14:30 If a revelation is made to another sitting by, let the first be silent. This only belabors the obvious. If one speaks, the other must listen in silence. All civilized and, I dare say, many "uncivilized" societies, take this for granted. Where it does not maintain, chaos reigns. The requisite courtesy of listening to the other in silence is not an insignificant factor in building up the community.

14:31–32 For you can all prophesy one by one, so that all may learn and all be encouraged; and the spirits of prophets are subject to prophets. Paul keeps insisting on the "one-by-one" rule, for it is indispensable if prophecy is to discharge its function of "upbuilding and encouragement and consolation" (14:3). The charismatic prophet builds up the church by edifying, encouraging, and consoling each of its members. If an added reason were needed for the orderly discharge of the prophetic charism, "so that all may learn and all be encouraged," then this one-by-one rule must surely be it.

The addition of "the spirits of prophets are subject to prophets" need mean no more than the other prophets present not only keep silence but attend to what one of them is saying. Prophets can learn from and be edified by one another. The perennial caricature of this exhortation is in those who organize lectures, courses, retreats, or what have you, for those entrusted to their pastoral care, while they themselves absent themselves from profiting by them. All too often, they stand in more need of what they recommend to others than any of their subjects. Being a prophet is no excuse for disdain of learning. "Love learning," wrote Saint Augustine to Consentius, "ardently." In the Christian community, perhaps as in no other, "faith comes from what is heard" (Rom 10:17).

14:33a For God is not a God of confusion but of peace. This statement merely makes explicit the overarching principle that determines the conduct of everyone in the Christian assembly. God is the Creator who brought order (*cosmos*) out of confusion (*chaos*). Order is the peace that God, and only God, brings into the world.

It ill becomes the "glad tidings" of this peace to be proclaimed midst warring factions, conflicting claims and interests, and confusion. Paul's reminder of this fundamental truth about God must surely have been brought about by the disruptive behavior of members of the Corinthian church when the community gathered to eat the Supper of the Lord. No one, however, can be so sanguine as to believe that this problem was confined to the church of Corinth. It must have been then, and still is now, pandemic.

14:33b–34 As in all the churches of the saints, the women should keep silence in the churches. For they are not permitted to speak, but should be subordinate, as even the law says. Very controversial though this passage be, a few comments on it are called for. First of all, Paul is not inventing a rule of conduct—and this is all it is—but only reminding the Corinthians of a practice common to "all the churches of the saints." Second, having already enjoined silence on men in the assembly (14:28, 30, 34), Paul now directs his attention to the women there. Why this should rouse so much controversy when the other did not is incomprehensible. Third, men have been the cause of confusion (14:33) and disorder when the community came together as a church (11:18); it is surely not beyond the realm of the possible that so have women. Finally, as his Jewish upbringing had taught him and so many other converts to Christianity like him in the churches of the saints, the law in Genesis 3:16, "He shall rule over you," was not taken lightly nor disregarded easily. Who, then, all these centuries later, can honestly point an accusing finger at Paul for saying this?

14:35 If there is anything they desire to know, let them ask their husbands at home. For it is shameful for a woman to speak in church. Asking for enlightenment on a given point from someone whose opinion you value is no more shameful for a man than it is for a woman. So, the first part of the verse can give no genuine offense save to those predisposed to be offended, perhaps for reasons that have little or nothing to do with what Paul is talking about.

The second part of the verse, the "it is shameful for a woman to speak in church," should be seen against Paul's own background, not elevated to the status of a Sinaitic commandment. In the chapter on marriage problems (1 Cor 7), we saw Paul, in full cognizance of an explicit command of the Lord himself on divorce, go diametrically contrary to its prohibition (compare 7:10–11 with 7:12–13). Why, then, must Paul's own statement prohibiting women to speak in church be taken any more inalterably than a command of the Lord? Once again, Christians need to be reminded that the New Testament is simply not that kind of a book. It does not substitute a new set of laws for old ones.

14:36 What! Did the word of God originate with you, or are you the only ones it has reached? This is a conclusion not to the immediate section on women's conduct in church but to the whole chapter's dealing with the Word, whether uttered in tongues, in prophecy, or in teaching. No one church and no single individual in any church possesses a monopoly on the Word of God. It is God's Word, and no one else's. Its origin is God, and God alone. Therefore, Paul's statement can just as well be addressed to any number of today's churches who act as though the Word of God were their own exclusive preserve, as though they alone are the arbiters of its meaning. To them Paul says, with even more justification than he did to the Corinthians, "What! Did the word of God originate with you, or are you the only ones it has reached?"

14:37 If any one thinks that he is a prophet, or spiritual, he should acknowledge that what I am writing to you is a command of the Lord. Such a concluding remark is, in a sense, a reiteration of the criteria of the charisms. Paul addresses the prophets and a broader category of those who claim "to have spiritual powers" [NRSV], anyone who is a *pneumatikos*. What he reminds such individuals here is a variant of the first criterion for the use of the charisms, the criterion of orthodox confession (12:3). The command of the Lord, of course, embraces the end of all charisms: the common good (12:17) and edification (14:27).

14:38 If any one does not recognize this, he is not recognized. This, as it were, is a traditional prophetic conclusion. It follows from the fact that what Paul has said about the use of the charismatic gifts in the church is in fact a command of the Lord. The formulaic threat (for example, Deut 4:2; Jer 11:3; 1 Thess 4:8; Rev 22:18–19) here is a reminder that those who do not recognize the teaching as a command of the Lord are, in turn, themselves not recognized. This is the reverse side of what Paul said in 8:3, "But if one loves God, one is known by him" (see the previous remarks on 8:3; and on 11:16, 19).

14:39 So, my brethren, earnestly desire to prophesy, and do not forbid speaking in tongues;... After all that Paul has said on prophecy and speaking in tongues, after juxtaposing them as spiritual gifts and awarding the preference to the former, it is only natural that he add this reminder. He warns those who possess the charism of prophecy not to disparage those who speak in tongues nor to forbid them to do so. In the church, there is ample room for the diversity and the multiplicity of all the innumerable charisms needed by the Body of Christ, however outré some might seem.

14:40 but all things should be done decently and in order. That the great many spiritual gifts enjoyed by the members of the body should attain their appointed end, the edification of the body, it is necessary that they function harmoniously and in an orderly fashion. That "all things should be done decently and in order" is nothing but the criterion of the common good writ large. This, after all, is what Paul means when he reminds the Romans, "To set the mind on the Spirit is life and peace" (Rom 8:6).

Chapter 15

FIRST CORINTHIANS 15

15:1–2 Now I would remind you, brethren, in what terms I preached to you the gospel,... When all is said and done, back to the gospel must we go. Whatever the crises you face, go back to the gospel. Contrary to all the prevailing views and attitudes, faith and salvation in Jesus Christ are in the life of the gospel and nowhere else, certainly not in the clever manipulation of cases of conscience, nor in the multiplicity of decrees and interdictions, let alone postmodern theories of redemption.

It is wholly understandable that Paul should pay attention to the problems facing the Corinthians in their daily living of the gospel. It is inevitable that, in their life with one another, frictions and conflicts should arise. If Paul attended to all of them, it was primarily to facilitate for a nascent Christian community their attention and attachment to the gospel, to the glad tidings of Jesus Christ, "whom God made our wisdom, our righteousness and sanctification and redemption" (1:30). The tragedy in all this is that long after the churches were established, the solution of problems and responses to queries became the established procedure, and the gospel itself was left to languish in pious preachments and spiritual exhortations.

If today's church stands in need of anything, it is precisely the need for the gospel. It has this in common with the church in Corinth, and with every other church in Christendom. It does not need fulminations, multiplication of edicts, or newfangled moral solutions to fabricated dilemmas. In every age, the church needs to be reminded again and again of the simple and unalterable gospel that was preached from the dawn of the first Easter.

which you received, in which you stand, by which you are saved, if you hold it fast—unless you believed in vain. Life, true life in Christ, means simply the acceptance of and the perseverance in the gospel of salvation. Not even the Almighty could compel assent to the free gift of life in Christ. Such a gift is freely given and must as freely be accepted and, in the very instance of its acceptance, gratefully acknowledged for what it truly is: an unearned and unmerited gift. This set of relationships, as we have had occasion to note previously, is what Paul understood by grace.

Such gratefully acknowledged acceptance ("which you received") of the gospel is never a once-for-all act but embraces the entire life of the total person ("in which you stand"). Only by this tenacious adherence to the gospel ("if you hold it fast") does the believer possess that single most precious gift of God, true life in Christ ("by which you are saved"). Therefore, it is all too readily understandable why Paul, having passed in review so many and such different problems besetting the newly founded church in Corinth, comes at last to the one single valid response to all questions and queries. This is why one of the greatest modern interpreters of the New Testament titled his commentary on First Corinthians *The Resurrection of the Dead*, the subject of this chapter.

That Paul adds, "unless you believed in vain," is a rhetorical way of accentuating precisely the opposite: Their faith has not been in vain! The Corinthians' faith, for all the tribulations and trials it was passing through, stood unshaken. Cardinal Newman aptly remarked, "Ten thousand difficulties do not make a doubt." Would that today's church had someone to remind it, mid today's "inspissated gloom," that its faith, too, is not in vain; else, our prayer at the Eucharist, "Look not upon our sins but on the faith of your church," would have fallen on deaf ears.

15:3 For I delivered to you as of first importance what I also received,... The classic formula of tradition is like that which introduced the institution of the Lord's Supper, "For I received from the Lord what I also delivered to you" (11:23). Important though that formula was, this one is "of first importance." It is, as the Greek vocable has it, first, foremost, most important, because it hands on the gospel. Paul "received" it, he did not invent it. His being the apostle he is bears witness to his utter fidelity in transmitting what he himself had received. This is true of all the apostles, all the evangelists, the missionaries, the preachers and the teachers of the gospel in every age. Fidelity to handing on the tradition is the prime responsibility of all who proclaim the gospel.

The utter simplicity of this gospel is what demands this utmost fidelity in its transmission and its reception. Those who object that the times have changed and we with them imagine the gospel to be other than the stark and simple statement that follows:

that Christ died for our sins in accordance with the scriptures,...
The first article of this creed is in two parts: "that Christ died," a historically verifiable fact; and "for our sins," a faith understanding of the fact. Since you hardly need the Scriptures to prove that someone died, the "in accordance with the scriptures" must be, therefore, confirmatory of the "for our sins." In all likelihood, the Scriptures that the formula has in mind is Isaiah:

> Surely he has borne our griefs and carried our sorrows; yet we esteemed him stricken, smitten by God, and afflicted. But he was wounded for our transgressions, he was bruised for our iniquities; upon him was the chastisement that made us whole, and with his stripes we are healed. All we like sheep have gone astray; we have turned every one to his own way; and the Lord has laid on him the iniquity of us all. (Isa 53:4–6)
> By oppression and judgment he was taken away; and as for his generation, who considered that he was cut off out of the land of the living, stricken for the transgression of my people? And they made his grave with the wicked and with a rich man in his death, although

he had done no violence, and there was no deceit in his mouth. (53:8–9)

Therefore I will divide him a portion with the great, and he shall divide the spoil with the strong; because he poured out his soul to death, and was numbered with the transgressors; yet he bore the sin of many, and made intercession for the transgressors. (53:12)

What is often overlooked, however, in the "for our sins" is the indispensable acknowledgment of our own sins and, consequently, of our need to be delivered from them. The reason this fundamental article of the faith is relegated to the margin nowadays is simply our reluctance to speak of sin at all or to admit that we are all sinners. Needless to say, if you have no sin, believing in anybody dying for our sins is meaningless. Hide sin from view, and the redemption by the death of Christ is relegated to a negligible position, somewhere well behind anthropology, sociology, and ecology.

15:4 that he was buried, that he was raised on the third day in accordance with the scriptures,... The second part of this formula, the oldest we have in the New Testament, except perhaps the formula in Romans 1:1–4, "the gospel concerning his Son," holds the key to the whole gospel.

That "he was buried" is neither a reference to the empty tomb nor a proof of the resurrection. That the tomb where the crucified Jesus was buried was empty means no more than that the tomb was empty. There could be innumerable explanations for this, but none of them necessitated the resurrection of the occupant from the dead. In fact, Matthew has preserved one such possible explanation:

> And when they had assembled with the elders and taken counsel, they gave a sum of money to the soldiers and said, "Tell people, 'His disciples came by night and stole him away while we were asleep.' And if this comes to the governor's ears, we will satisfy him and keep you

out of trouble." So they took the money and did as they were directed; and this story has been spread among the Jews to this day. (Matt 28:12–15)

No, the "he was buried," far from being here a proof of the resurrection is a confirmation of the fact of death. This is all the more necessary to keep in mind because real death is the one necessary condition for true resurrection from the dead: "What you sow does not come to life unless it dies" (15:36).

The "that he was raised on the third day" is, again, an object of faith, in the same category as the "for us" in the previous verse. The "in accordance with the scriptures" is, in this context, problematic. There is, strictly speaking, no scriptural text that bears out this particular statement. It is generally presumed, however, that the reference is to one of two loci, or perhaps to both:

After two days he will revive us; on the third day he will raise us up, that we may live before him. (Hos 6:2)

Then Jonah prayed to the Lord his God from the belly of the fish, saying, "I called to the Lord, out of my distress, and he answered me; out of the belly of Sheol I cried, and you heard my voice." (Jonah 2:1–2)

We have to keep in mind that the "belly of Sheol" in Jonah is a reference to the realm of the dead. But a better argument can be made for "in accordance with the scriptures" being a reference to the "on the third day" implied in Hosea's "after two days."

One may well wonder if the "in accordance with the scriptures" is not a mnemonic device to help the faithful remember the credal formula. Parallel structures, such as we find in verses 3 and 4 here, are a common enough mnemonic device in, for instance, the psalms. But the number of days is not the essential here, and not too much should be made of it, however serviceable it has proved to be in the liturgy.

15:5 and that he appeared to Cephas, then to the twelve. This is the "fact" to which the faith in "he was raised" corresponds. The fact is that Cephas and the twelve had an experience that, they themselves said, made them believe that Jesus was raised from the dead. Yet, even this has to be understood in the light of Jesus' words to Thomas, "Blessed are those who have not seen and yet believe" (John 20:29). This, of course, is true of Cephas, of the twelve, and of anyone who believes in the resurrection of Jesus.

The reason why this is so is simply that the resurrection is, by its very nature as an eschatological phenomenon, one that belongs to the world to come, and is consequently not the object of ocular vision. What Cephas and all the others said they saw was not Jesus of Nazareth, but "the Lord." The Lord is not and cannot in fact be the object of ocular vision (see John 1:18; 5:37; 1 John 4:12; 1 Tim 1:17). This, by the way, is the reason why Mary Magdalene (John 20:14), the disciples on the road to Emmaus (Luke 24:16), and all those privileged with Easter appearances had their "eyes kept from recognizing him." The simple fact of the matter is that, to recognize the risen Lord, you need a revelation. Revelation is an object of faith, not a conclusion to a syllogism.

15:6 Then he appeared to more than five hundred brethren at one time, most of whom are still alive, though some have fallen asleep. In the catalog of Easter appearances, this appearance to "more than five hundred" is of special importance. Although what happened on that occasion and how it happened eludes us, the point Paul is trying to make is that some of those so privileged "have fallen asleep." This is precisely the problem that occupied the Corinthians. It is not that they doubted the resurrection of Jesus but that they questioned the resurrection of the dead, which is the problem that Paul addresses in this chapter. One can well understand the Corinthians' dilemma: some who encountered the risen Lord have in fact died.

15:7 Then he appeared to James, then to all the apostles. The elenchus of the appearances is a bit puzzling. Was James one of "the twelve" (Mark 1:19; 3:17–18; 5:37; Gal 1:19; 2:9), already mentioned with Cephas in 1 Corinthians 15:5? Were not those twelve themselves apostles? Whatever the explanation, there is an evidently good reason why Paul added "all the apostles" at this juncture. He wants to insist he is one of their number: "Am I not an apostle? Have I not seen Jesus our Lord?" (1 Cor 9:1). Nevertheless, Paul's problem here is not that of the author of Acts, who reminds us that the risen Jesus was made "manifest; *not to all the people* but to us who were chosen by God as witnesses, who ate and drank with him after he rose from the dead" (Acts 10:41). Had the encounter been an ocular phenomenon, Acts would never have been able to make such a statement.

15:8 *Last of all, as to one untimely born, he appeared also to me.* The list of appearances has been advancing steadily toward this proof of Paul's status as an apostle. The puzzling thing is whether "last of all" merely indicates Paul's place in the line or marks the absolute conclusion to the series. From the rest of the argument employed by Paul, the former is the more likely interpretation. One may legitimately ask, however, whether the narrative of resurrection events at the end of Luke and the beginning of Acts was somehow deliberately meant to exclude Paul from—to Luke's mind at least—the restricted category of "apostle." If this be so, then Luke is merely reflecting a prejudice already existing in Paul's lifetime (1 Cor 1:1; Gal 1:1).

A word about "as to one untimely born." This is perhaps a reference to the traditional prophetic vocation of Isaiah (49:1) and Jeremiah (1:5), which Paul himself echoes in the account of his own prophetic vocation in Galatians 1:15: "But when he who had set me apart before I was born, and had called me through his grace...." If this be so, then this is by no means an inappropriate place for Paul to remind his readers of his own calling.

15:9 *For I am the least of the apostles, unfit to be called an apostle, because I persecuted the church of God.* One could almost hear Paul add, *sotto voce*, "The least, the most unfit, and yet an apostle nevertheless!" But we must not dismiss lightly the compunction in his confession, "I persecuted the church of God." Those who in our day find great sport in this exercise will do well to ponder not only Paul's genuine repentance but the lifetime he spent in expiating his guilt. The gravity of "persecuted the church of God" can only be appreciated in the light of what Paul says about the Body of Christ.

15:10 But by the grace of God I am what I am, and his grace toward me was not in vain. On the contrary, I worked harder than any of them, though it was not I, but the grace of God which is with me. Not the least attractive of Paul's qualities is this genuine humility amid acknowledged triumph. He recognizes his own achievements and, in the very act, attributes them to their true source, "the grace of God." Saint Augustine echoes this in "I am holy because you sanctified me; because I received, not because I possessed; because you gave, not because I merited." Paul reveals that everything he is, he is solely by this grace. This is what we meant when we said that the life of the minister is no less eloquent a sermon than the gospel she or he proclaims. Both the life lived and the gospel proclaimed are witness to grace.

Paul's statement here is all the more important because it holds the key to the freedom of everyone who proclaims the Word: God's grace in them is never in vain; their labors are not solitary undertakings; and the final outcome is always a monument to God's grace, not to personal aggrandizement. Constant recognition of grace in our lives is sufficient to dispel any temptation to nullify the gift by denying its gratuity.

15:11 Whether then it was I or they, so we preach and so you believed. Regardless of who preached the good news to them, it was the same gospel that was preached and the same that was believed, the same gospel that was received and the same that was delivered to them. When all is said and done, everything else is a distraction from this gospel of Jesus Christ.

15:12 Now if Christ is preached as raised from the dead, how can some of you say that there is no resurrection of the dead? We have come here to the point at issue. In affirming the gospel of Christ's death for our sins and his resurrection from the dead, Paul is setting the stage for addressing the problem that weighed on the Corinthians' minds. In reciting the Creed at the beginning of the chapter, he only reminded them of what they already believed. This was not in question at all. What was in question was the fate of the believer after death. What the Corinthians failed to see was the necessary link between Christ's resurrection and their own.

15:13 But if there is no resurrection of the dead, then Christ has not been raised;... Ordinary common sense dictates this. What the Corinthians need to keep in mind is precisely how the resurrection of Christ fits into the resurrection of the dead.

We often forget that the indispensable condition for any resurrection appearance was precisely a prior faith in the resurrection of the dead. "Seeing" Jesus after his death and burial is open to many explanations. None of them, however, necessitates concluding to his resurrection from the dead. When the risen Jesus reveals himself, then the disciple so privileged by this revelation must be already someone who believes that he too will one day rise. This is why, as was noted previously (on 15:7), Peter says that God raised Jesus up "on the third day and made him manifest; not to all the people but to us who were chosen by God as witnesses" (Acts 10:40–41). Prior faith in the resurrection of the dead is the necessary condition for faith in the resurrection of Christ.

15:14 if Christ has not been raised, then our preaching is in vain and your faith is in vain. Without the gospel of the resurrection, both preaching and the faith are in vain, for they lack any substance. As Saint Augustine reminded his flock, "Faith is not required to believe that Christ died, but it is required to believe that he rose from the dead."

15:15 We are even found to be misrepresenting God, because we testified of God that he raised Christ, whom he did not raise if it is true that the dead are not raised. If there were no resurrection of the dead, then the Christian kerygma, the proclamation of the Christian message, had to be a lie, because at the very heart of it is the resurrection of Christ. If, indeed, there were no resurrection of the dead, then Christ himself would not have been raised from the dead, and the good news of his resurrection could have been nothing but a fabrication. It is because God raises all the dead that he raised Christ; and, because he raised Christ, God raises all who die.

15:16 For if the dead are not raised, then Christ has not been raised. This reiterates and resumes the same argument. Christ's resurrection is one instance of the resurrection of the dead. The primary datum of faith in Christ's resurrection is the belief in the resurrection of the dead. Thus, for example, the Sadducees, who "say that there is no resurrection" (Acts 23:8; Matt 22:23), could not possibly believe that Jesus is risen from the dead. They were "annoyed because Peter and John were teaching the people and proclaiming in Jesus the resurrection from the dead" (Acts 4:2). In other words, to say Jesus is risen implies there is a resurrection from the dead, and vice versa.

15:17 If Christ has not been raised, your faith is futile and you are still in your sins. We now come to the saving aspect of the resurrection. Paul extends this line of rhetorical arguments in which the conclusion of one becomes the premise of the next: There is no resurrection of the dead; therefore, there is no resurrection of Christ; therefore, there is no forgiveness of sins. You simply cannot separate the "he died for our sins" from the "he was raised" in the credal formula in 15:3–4. Both together are necessary for the remission of sins. The salvation event is constituted by the death and the resurrection of Christ, not singly, but together as an inseparable unit. Christ's victory over death in his resurrection is what takes away our sins.

15:18 Then those also who have fallen asleep in Christ have perished. This is what was bothering the Corinthians. It is why Paul, in listing those privileged with an Easter appearance, felt it necessary to add, "Some have fallen asleep" (15:6). What of those who in the interim have also "fallen asleep," that is, died? Had there been no resurrection of the dead, then they too will have "perished." By the way, the Greek word for this circumlocution for death, "to fall asleep" (*koimaomai*), is where English derives "cemetery," which is in fact a "dormitory."

An often overlooked point in this verse is that Paul does not say, as we would be inclined to say, "those also who have fallen asleep" suffer eternal punishment in hell. Nothing could have been farther removed from his mind and the Corinthians'. What he says is simply that they have perished, ceased to be, have neither life nor existence anywhere.

15:19 If for this life only we have hoped in Christ, we are of all men most to be pitied. One may well try to sell this idea to some of our contemporaries, even those among them who profess the Christian faith. If, indeed, there is no "pie in the sky," then we deserve all the scorn the world heaps on us. If Christ had not conquered death and given us a life that is not and will never be under the shadow of death, an eternal life, then we are the biggest fools on the face of the earth. Pity, in that instance, would be wasted on us.

15:20 But in fact Christ has been raised from the dead, the first fruits of those who have fallen asleep. No one could possibly miss the note of triumph here. Not only has Christ "been raised from the dead," but, in having been raised, he is the "first fruits," the first instance that constitutes all the others, of all who die. Christ's resurrection from the dead is all the proof any believer needs that those who die in Christ shall not perish. Christ, in other words, is at the head of a new creation.

15:21 For as by a man came death, by a man has come also the resurrection of the dead. Here and in Romans 5:12, we have the start of the argument of the "two Adams." We have to keep in mind that, after the Genesis account (Gen 3—5), the figure of Adam is hardly ever mentioned in the Old Testament (Josh 3:16 and 1 Chr

1:1). It is in the intertestamental literature, the so-called apocalyptic literature, that Adam comes once again to the fore, because that literature was marked by a division of time into this world and the world to come. In the world to come, the drama will be replayed. There will be a new Adam, a new Seth, a new Enoch, and so on. This apocalyptic genre of writing happened to be the popular literature of the day in the time of Jesus and Paul. Out of that literature, Paul chose the figure of Adam as a foil to that of Christ, the new Adam.

Paul, moreover, often thinks in binary opposites. Thus, from the figure of Christ he argues back to Adam, and not vice versa, as so many theologians are wont to do. If in Christ death is conquered, then in Adam death must have had its origin. If in Christ sin is forgiven, then in Adam sin came into the world. If in Christ we have been set free, then from Adam we inherit our bondage.

It is hard to improve on Saint Augustine's summation of the two Adams:

> In the history of these two men, one of whom lost all of us by doing his own will and not that of his Creator, and the other saved us by doing, not his own will, but that of him who sent him, in the history of these two men, the entire Christian faith consists.

15:22 *For as in Adam all die, so also in Christ shall all be made alive.* The argument, in fact, is in reverse. Paul knows and firmly believes that in Christ we have life; therefore, at the beginning in Adam we came to know death. As Romans puts it, "Therefore as sin came into the world through one man and death through sin, and so death spread to all men because all men sinned" (Rom 5:12). The link of death to sin is peculiar to Paul. It is not a notion found in the Old Testament. As a matter of fact, in the Genesis account, death is not so much part of a punishment as the end of, the relief from, the punishment due to Adam's sins: "In the sweat of your face you shall eat bread *till* you return to the ground, for out of it you were taken; you are dust, and to dust you shall return" (Gen 3:19).

In the long history of original sin, Romans 5:12 has, alas, received scant attention. Both its assertions are unqualified. In Adam, *all* die, all without exception; just as all without exception "shall be made alive" in Christ. Indeed one is hard pressed to conjure anything as remotely universal as the "all die" that is the consequence of Adam's trespass.

15:23 But each in his own order: Christ the first fruits, then at his coming those who belong to Christ. Just as the resurrection of the dead is the necessary condition for the resurrection of Christ, so, too, the resurrection of Christ is the necessary condition for the resurrection of those who belong to him. This is what his being the "first fruits" means. His resurrection reveals the fact of what could have only been a hope till then. Christ's resurrection is the proof that death itself has been definitively conquered (1 Cor 15:55).

Immediately, the question of when crops up. Paul's answer, alas, is not much help. He simply says, "At his coming" (*parousia*). But, to him, that meant an event in the proximate future, which he expected even in his own lifetime (1 Thess 5:17). Of course, he was wrong, and so were many of his generation. Centuries and millennia have passed, and the question remains. Its only possible answer is that we do not know. But, then, neither did Jesus himself: "But of that day and hour no one knows, not even the angels of heaven, nor the Son, but the Father only" (Matt 24:36; see 1 Thess 5:1–2).

15:24 Then comes the end, when he delivers the kingdom to God the Father after destroying every rule and every authority and power. The final triumph of Christ over every "rule, authority and power" only makes clear "you are Christ's, and Christ is God's" (3:23). Faith in the resurrection means a firm and unshakable belief in Christ's final triumph over all that, to us, seems immovable and doomed to seeming permanence. What we all forget is that the overthrow of the "rule, authority and power" extends not just to worldly powers but to the church itself when it takes on aspects of the world. At the resurrection, God will be "all in all" (15:28 NRSV). Therefore, "let no one boast of men" (3:21), though they be enthroned and mitred, robed in purple, or conquerors of continents. If there is a resurrection of the dead, then there is bound to be a restoration of perspective, where finally "many that are first will be last, and the last first" (Mark 10:31).

15:25 For he must reign until he has put all his enemies under his feet. This must necessarily take a very long time. It is what tests, from one generation to another, the faith of those who belong to Christ. They pray daily "Thy kingdom come," unaware that the process is protracted over centuries. Their faith is the only guarantee they possess that, in every age, the enemies of Christ, their spectacular triumphs and unsustainable boasts notwithstanding, are being put "under his feet." Yet, because of their ignorance of the extent of the "until," those who belong to Christ find, not so much their faith, as their hope being subjected to severe temptations. One would have thought that, as a necessary consequence, hope constitutes one of the topics regularly preached to the community of Christ; and yet it is not. No wonder so many Christians consult the daily horoscope.

15:26 The last enemy to be destroyed is death. All religions of salvation have to wrestle with salvation from death. It is, in fact, the only absolute in life, despite all the claims of quacks, ancient and modern. We do not need all the abundant reminders of its finality, its irreversibility, its inevitability. Faith in the resurrection means that, nevertheless, death does not have the last word. The last word belongs exclusively to him who conquered death.

The mistake many make is to confound death with dying. Christ himself died. His dying conquered death, conquered the dominion of death, not the fact of dying. We all still "owe God a death." Like Christ, we must die in order to be raised from the dead. Those who belong to Christ are not, and cannot, therefore, be exempt from dying. Christ's resurrection means that their death is not the last act. It is, rather, the necessary condition for a life that never again comes under the shadow of death: "For we know that Christ being raised from the dead will never die again; death no longer has dominion over him" (Rom 6:9).

15:27 "For God has put all things in subjection under his feet." But when it says, "All things are put in subjection under him," it is plain that he is excepted who put all things under him. As is his wont, Paul now cites the Scriptures to cap his argument. His citing Psalm 110:1, one of the christological psalms most frequently cited in the entire New Testament, is quite significant. The author of the event of salvation, lest it be forgotten, is God the Father. This is why Paul goes to the trouble of making this clear in his interpretation of the verse.

15:28 When all things are subjected to him, then the Son himself will also be subjected to him who put all things under him, that God may be everything to every one [NRSV: so that God may be all in all]. The subjection of all things to the Son is of a different order from his own subjection to the Father. The reign, the kingdom that Christ inaugurated by his coming into the world, was the necessary step to be taken in order to bring all things under the dominion of the Father. The creation that was, to paraphrase Pascal, shattered by disobedience in the first garden, Eden, is restored to wholeness by obedience in the second, Gethsemane.

The subjection of all things to the Son is a subservience. His dominion subjects them all "under his feet." At the same time, his subjection to the Father, far from being subservience, is filial obedience. Contrary to the common misconception, genuine obedience is never subservience, but a means of union, an expression of love. This obedience of the Son is what revealed God as Father, so that God will indeed be "all in all," the "one God, the Father, from whom are all things and for whom we exist, and one Lord, Jesus Christ, through whom are all things and through whom we exist" (1 Cor 8:6).

15:29 Otherwise, what do people mean by being baptized on behalf of the dead? If the dead are not raised at all, why are people baptized on their behalf? If the Corinthians did indeed grasp the connection of this statement with what preceded, and if they did comprehend what Paul is talking about here, today's readers are not so fortunate. Despite all the attempts of expert interpreters, this verse remains shrouded in impenetrable obscurity. All that can be guessed at now is that Paul himself considers it as another argument for the resurrection of the dead.

15:30 Why am I in peril every hour? Though the question is clearly rhetorical, and Paul expects his readers to respond to it spontaneously, today's readers, alas, are not so clairvoyant. The nexus with the previous verse seems tenuous at best, and this only compounds the difficulty of interpretation.

15:31 I protest, brethren, by my pride in you which I have in Christ Jesus our Lord, I die every day! The protestation of his pride in them is genuine. For, despite all the problems besetting them, the Corinthian church was indeed a church to be proud of, on condition that the pride be grounded in Christ Jesus our Lord. In saying this, Paul is only practicing what he preaches: "Let him who boasts, boast of the Lord" (1 Cor 1:31; 2 Cor 10:17).

The "I die every day" could be no more than a reminder that genuine ministry entails death to self. In that resounding peroration to Romans 8, Paul cites Psalm 44:22: "For your sake we are being killed all the day long; we are regarded as sheep to be slaughtered" (Rom 8:36). It is quite likely that Paul has the same psalm in mind in 1 Corinthians 15:31 also.

15:32 What do I gain if, humanly speaking, I fought with beasts at Ephesus? If the dead are not raised, "Let us eat and drink, for tomorrow we die." Whether the "if" is real or hypothetical, what matters here is the apostle's facing death in all different occasions and circumstances. The precariousness of the life of the ministry, the perpetual exposure to death in all its forms, makes no sense whatever if when you die you simply die, period. "If the dead are not raised," then the patent squandering of one's life for others is arrant nonsense. "If for this life only we have hoped in Christ, we are of all men most to be pitied" (1 Cor 15:19). Then, the only thing that makes sense would be to plunge heedlessly into all the pleasures this life has to offer, "Let us eat and drink, for tomorrow we die" (Isa 22:13; Luke 12:19).

15:33 Do not be deceived: "Bad company ruins good morals." Many of the problems the Corinthians face are, like our own, the result of the "bad company" they keep: the incessant questioning, the endless challenge, the interminable criticism of those who not only do not share their faith but despise it. This quotation, by the way, is one of the very rare instances in the whole New Testament (about six in all) when a Greek literary work outside the Bible is cited. These words come from a fragment of a work by Menander (d. 290 BC) called *Thaïs*.

15:34 Come to your right mind, and sin no more. For some have no knowledge of God. I say this to your shame. The plea for a measure of sanity is understandable in the light of the "bad company" that, very likely, had no knowledge of God or his Christ. Association with this bad company is bound to put the faith of the Corinthians in jeopardy. Paul's admonition is to shame them into recognizing their error and turn to the God who "raised the Lord and will also raise us up by his power" (1 Cor 6:14).

15:35 But some one will ask, "How are the dead raised? With what kind of body do they come?" It is quite possible that the "some one" who asks this question is Paul himself, else why the circumlocution? To this question there can be only one possible answer: I do not know! Indeed, no one knows. But this did not stop Paul or those who came after him from attempting some answer, one more unconvincing than the other. The temptation is simply too strong to conceal one's ignorance. Paul succumbs to the temptation and attempts to answer the unanswerable question in every way imaginable.

There are two questions being asked: the question of the how, which is unanswerable; and the question of what kind of body is the resurrection body. This latter question is ambiguous because what is understood by "body" can itself be in question. If you read "body" as part of a body/soul dichotomy, which is hardly Pauline, you have to presuppose some form of the immortality of the soul. The question here is, Can you find any such "Platonic" body/soul understanding of the human person in Paul? If, however, you take "body" in its biblical sense as meaning the entire "I," then, because this "I" ceases to be in death, the resurrection body can only be a new creation.

15:36–38 You foolish man! [NRSV: Fool!] What you sow does not come to life unless it dies. And what you sow is not the body which is to be, but a bare kernel, perhaps of wheat or of some other grain. But God gives it a body as he has chosen, and to each kind of seed its own body. The first statement, "What you sow...," is unexceptionable. Although the image of "body" that follows it is elaborated here, in the final analysis, it leads nowhere. Note that verse 37 describes change of one thing into another: the "what you sow," "the bare kernel," and what that same kernel becomes. But this is not what Paul intends, for he adds, "God gives it a body as he has chosen," that is, a new creation. How else can God, who is ever the Creator out of nothing, act?

15:39–41 For not all flesh is alike, but there is one kind for men, another for animals, another for birds, and another for fish. There are celestial bodies and there are terrestrial bodies; but the glory of the celestial is one, and the glory of the terrestrial is another. There is one glory of the sun, and another glory of the moon, and another glory of the stars; for star differs from star in glory. Paul begins to draw on his extensive arsenal of imagery to try to formulate a nonexistent answer. Agricultural imagery gives way to taxonomy, which in turn cedes to astronomy, then metaphysics, and back to the creation of Adam. The imagery, for all its multiplicity, is impotent to convey what Paul wants to say.

Perhaps Paul's principal reason for failure—and this is no more than conjecture—is the line of argument he adopts. He presumes that the mortal body itself changes. Therefore, he must presume the continuance of one thing into another, for example, the seed into the plant. But what if, perhaps, just perhaps, the continuity was not on that level but rather on the level of relationships? Death would then put an end to the entire "I," body and soul and spirit. This "I" ceases to be. Then God, who always creates out of nothing, calls out of the nothing of death identifiably the same person, with all his or her relationships intact, the relationships to oneself, to others, and to God. The miracle of the resurrection would then be not bringing the dead to life but bringing back the identifiably same person, with all her or his relationships integral and intact. This, by the way, is the reason why, in the resurrection appearances, Jesus comes to his own in the daily intimacy of their past encounters with him, conversing with them, sharing their food, and reminding them of what he had taught them.

15:42–44 *So is it with the resurrection of the dead. What is sown is perishable, what is raised is imperishable. It is sown in dishonor, it is raised in glory. It is sown in weakness, it is raised in power. It is sown a physical body, it is raised a spiritual body. If there is a physical body, there is also a spiritual body.* What looks like an obvious conclusion is really not. What precisely is it concluding from, and to what? Speaking of a physical body might be a venial pleonasm, but to speak of a spiritual body is almost an oxymoron, a contradiction in terms. The argument concludes that the existence of one kind of body necessarily involves the existence of the other. But, then, what role does the resurrection play? Is death a transformation from one kind of body to another? Or is the resurrection a genuine new creation?

15:45–49 *Thus it is written, "The first man Adam became a living being"; the last Adam became a life-giving spirit. But it is not the spiritual which is first but the physical, and then the spiritual. The first man was from the earth, a man of dust; the second man is from heaven. As was the man of dust, so are those who are of the dust; and as is the man of heaven, so are those who are of heaven. Just as we have borne the image of the man of dust, we shall also bear the image of the man of heaven.* Sublime though this be, it is not very clear how it can provide the answer to "How are the dead raised? With what kind of body do they come?" (15:35). The contrast of the two Adams is a perfect statement of our redemption in Christ Jesus. That the "last Adam became a life-giving spirit" is a compendious confession of the new creation in Christ Jesus. It not only affirms the life-giving function of the Spirit but stresses the link between the Spirit and Christ the Lord. This, as has been said, is sublime Christology, but it leaves the question about the how of the resurrection and the kind of body that rises where we found it initially, in the penumbra of our ignorance.

15:50 I tell you this, brethren: flesh and blood cannot inherit the kingdom of God, nor does the perishable inherit the imperishable. The parallel is defective at best. That flesh and blood cannot inherit the kingdom of God is evident. But that the perishable does not inherit the imperishable, if it made any sense, is doubtful. These two categories, "perishable...imperishable," are not contrasted the way the first two, "flesh and blood...kingdom of God," are; nor can "inherit" mean the same thing in both statements.

15:51 Lo! I tell you a mystery. We shall not all sleep, but we shall all be changed... This is the very heart of the problem. All of Paul's futile attempts at an explanation must in the end come to this starting point. The how of the resurrection is a mystery and, therefore, defies explanation even if it ostensibly invites reflection. Paul's own reflection is subject to his unshakable conviction that he will live to see the end, the parousia of the Lord. Even here he makes his conviction—soon to be proven false—pathetically clear: "We shall not all sleep."

15:52 in a moment, in the twinkling of an eye, at the last trumpet. For the trumpet will sound, and the dead will be raised imperish-

able, and we shall be changed. This is clearly apocalyptic language, all too familiar to Paul and his contemporaries. The sobriety of expression, in contrast with the exuberance of the previous passage (15:36–50), is striking. Paul speaks here of "change" in a wholly different sense. This change underlines the radical alteration of the perishable to the imperishable. In other words, the resurrection life is the life one lives but never again under the shadow of death. Henceforth, the loves you had before now are the identical same loves, but they are no longer under the shadow of death. Instead of exercising the imagination on the protraction of time into eternity, as we are sometimes wont to do, we should try the nigh-impossible task of imagining what it would mean to love another person without being under the shadow of death. In the final analysis, that might provide us with a better hint of what Paul is talking about.

15:53 For this perishable nature must put on the imperishable, and this mortal nature must put on immortality. To add "nature" [RSV] or "body" [NRSV] is to complicate unnecessarily what is already a mystery. The Greek simply says, "For the corruptible shall put on incorruptibility and the mortal, immortality." Brief and concise, this formula sums up admirably the resurrection life. What distinguishes the creature from the Creator is precisely corruptibility, perishableness, mortality. God and God alone is immortal: "To the King of ages, immortal, invisible, the only God, be honor and glory for ever and ever. Amen" (1 Tim 1:17; Rom 1:23). The resurrection confers on the mortal creature that "lest you die" (Gen 3:3), which Adam and Eve wished to avoid by their primal disobedience. As Saint Augustine put it, in paradise they *could* not die (*posse non mori*); henceforth, they *couldn't* die (*non posse mori*).

15:54–55 When the perishable puts on the imperishable, and the mortal puts on immortality, then shall come to pass the saying that is written: "Death is swallowed up in victory." "O death, where is thy victory? O death, where is thy sting?" Recourse to Isaiah 25:8 and to Hosea 13:14 in their Greek Septuagintal versions is by way of bringing scriptural authority to bear on the argument for the definitive victory of resurrection life over death. The problem that beset humanity from the day of Abel, when the first tear was shed at the sight of death, receives in the resurrection its definitive solution for all who believe that Christ is risen from the dead. To inquire into the how of the process is to inquire too curiously indeed.

15:56 *The sting of death is sin, and the power of sin is the law.* Such a statement of our redemption in Christ could scarcely be bettered. That death came into the world through sin (Rom 5:12) is a primary datum of Pauline soteriology, his doctrine of salvation. But that "the sting of death is sin" is insufficiently reflected upon. The fact that we have to die is at the root of all our sins, whatever their nature or gravity. To desire to lay hold of life on my own terms, the forthright refusal to accept life as an utterly free gift of the Creator, makes me grasp for it, and thus sin. The "sting of death" is indeed sin.

A superlative means of deluding ourselves into laying hold of life is our adherence to the law. It enables us to separate the free gift of life from its giver by providing us with the illusion that we put God under obligation, making him indebted to us, and thereby denying the gratuity of his gift. By keeping the law we delude ourselves into believing that we earn the gift, and thus we sin, we offend against the giver. "Law came in, to increase the trespass" (Rom 5:20). "Now it is evident that no man is justified before God by the law" (Gal 3:11), and yet we are continually told that we are. Evidently, it requires a far greater than Paul to convince us that "the power of sin is the law."

15:57 *But thanks be to God, who gives us the victory through our Lord Jesus Christ.* This is the sole credible attitude in the presence of such a mystery as the resurrection. Rather than inquire into its inscrutable workings, accept the mystery with gratitude, the gratitude that can only be expressed in an act of faith. That the victory over death is ours can only be a gift of God through the redemptive death and resurrection of our Lord Jesus Christ.

15:58 Therefore, my beloved brethren, be steadfast, immovable, always abounding in the work of the Lord, knowing that in the Lord your labor is not in vain. The concluding exhortation scarcely needs expressing. Any attentive listener to Paul's letter thus far must grasp the need to "be steadfast, immovable," especially in the face of the world's determined opposition to Christ and to Christians and to all they stand for. But this steadfastness and immovableness is not a stasis. It requires the ceaseless dynamic of "the work of the Lord," which is love. It requires ministry to others throughout one's life. In this love and in its exercise in the ministry to others, we have all the reassurance we need that our labor is not "in vain": "But by the grace of God I am what I am, and his grace toward me was not in vain" (1 Cor 15:10; 2 Cor 6:1).

Chapter 16

FIRST CORINTHIANS 16

16:1 Now concerning the contribution for the saints: as I directed the churches of Galatia, so you also are to do. The last item on which the Corinthians sought enlightenment in their letter to Paul (1 Cor 7:1) had to do with a collection for the mother church in Jerusalem. Because of "a great famine" in the days of Emperor Claudius (AD 41–54), "the disciples determined, every one according to his ability, to send relief to the brethren who lived in Judea" (Acts 11:28–29). This is by no means an unfamiliar situation today. Nor is Paul's response to the Corinthians anything less than practical:

16:2 On the first day of every week, each of you is to put something aside and store it up, as he may prosper, so that contributions need not be made when I come. Not a bad idea for a Sunday exercise. Putting aside something each week, each according to her or his ability, would obviate the need of one large contribution when Paul comes. "For if the readiness is there, it is acceptable according to what a man has, not according to what he has not" (2 Cor 8:12).

What we risk missing here is Paul's reluctance to get embroiled in money matters, something which, alas, did not spare him later accusations: "We intend that no one should blame us about this liberal gift which we are administering" (2 Cor 8:20). One would have thought that, at least, he left behind him an important attitude and a valuable lesson to follow.

16:3–4 And when I arrive, I will send those whom you accredit by letter to carry your gift to Jerusalem. If it seems advisable that I should go also, they will accompany me. Once again, the sensitivity with which Paul handles the matter is striking. The donors, the Corinthians themselves, will have to see to the conveyance of their generous gift to Jerusalem. Paul merely offers his services "if it seems advisable." Later on, when writing to the Romans, he pays the Corinthians as handsome a tribute for their loving generosity as could be wished:

> At present, however, I am going to Jerusalem with aid for the saints. For Macedonia and Achaia have been pleased to make some contribution for the poor among the saints at Jerusalem; they were pleased to do it, and indeed they are in debt to them, for if the Gentiles have come to share in their spiritual blessings, they ought also to be of service to them in material blessings. (Rom 15:25–27)

16:5–9 I will visit you after passing through Macedonia, for I intend to pass through Macedonia, and perhaps I will stay with you or even spend the winter, so that you may speed me on my journey, wherever I go. For I do not want to see you now just in passing; I hope to spend some time with you, if the Lord permits. But I will stay in Ephesus until Pentecost, for a wide door for effective work has opened to me, and there are many adversaries. It is hard to imagine a reader of this concluding section of First Corinthians who has not either received from, or written a similar letter to, a loved one. Note how, as a believer, Paul qualifies his intention to "spend some time" with them by adding, "if the Lord permits" (see Jas 4:13–15; and previously on 1 Cor 4:19).

16:10–11 When Timothy comes, see that you put him at ease among you, for he is doing the work of the Lord, as I am. So let no one despise him. Speed him on his way in peace, that he may return to me; for I am expecting him with the brethren. How matter of fact is the recommendation of his "fellow-worker" (Rom 16:21), his "beloved and faithful child in the Lord" (1 Cor 4:17). The care to ease the path for one who is "doing the work of the Lord" set a good example for future generations, as witness the vast number of missionary correspondence that have come down to us over the centuries.

16:12 As for our brother Apollos, I strongly urged him to visit you with the other brethren, but it was not at all his will to come now. He will come when he has opportunity. The discreet respect for Apollos's own decision ("It was not at all his will to come now") is not only a proof of affection but also a sign of esteem for a brother in the ministry (1 Cor 3:6).

16:13 Be watchful, stand firm in your faith, be courageous, be strong. All these are part of the panoply of vigilance every Christian has to have in this world. One would have thought that Paul is belaboring the obvious. He is. But the Christian community, for all its knowledge of these things, stands in constant need of a reminder of the consolation of earnest exhortation to watchfulness, to steadfastness in the faith, to courage and strength in the face of the incessant assaults of its mighty enemies, the enemies of Christ and of Christians, that is, the world and all its agents, both inside and outside the church.

16:14 Let all that you do be done in love. We always have to come back to this, the one single mode of existence for the Christian: the existence in love. This is what Saint Augustine will echo in his commentary on First John: "Love and do what you will!" The Christian needs no other law, no other directive. Christian tradition has preserved the image of the beloved disciple in advanced old age, being carried in a chair around Ephesus. All he said was, "Little children, love one another!"

16:15–18 Now, brethren, you know that the household of Stephanas were the first converts in Achaia, and they have devoted themselves to the service of the saints; I urge you to be subject to such men and to every fellow worker and laborer. I rejoice at the coming of Stephanas and Fortunatus and Achaicus, because they have made up for your absence; for they refreshed my spirit as well as yours. Give recognition to such men. The exhortation to be subject to the leaders of the community is only fundamental common sense (see 1 Thess 5:12–13). It is one of the things to be done in love, not in servility and fear. For there can be "no fear in love, but perfect love casts out fear. For fear has to do with punishment, and he who fears is not perfected in love" (1 John 4:18).

The trio of "Stephanas and Fortunatus and Achaicus" must have been those who brought news of the Corinthians to Paul in Ephesus. It is very likely that a number of issues raised by Paul in First Corinthians prior to his mention of the letter he received from Corinth (1 Cor 7:1) were those brought to his attention by these three.

16:19 The churches of Asia send greetings. Aquila and Prisca, together with the church in their house, send you hearty greetings in the Lord. Aquila and Prisca are well known from the Book of Acts, "a Jew named Aquila, a native of Pontus, lately come from Italy with his wife Priscilla, because Claudius had commanded all the Jews to leave Rome" (Acts 18:2); from Romans, "Prisca and Aquila, my fellow workers in Christ Jesus" (Rom 16:3); and here. The "church in their house" could very well have been the house church where the Lord's Supper was celebrated (1 Cor 11:17–34). It takes little intelligence to reach the conclusion that as heads of the household, one of them must have presided at the celebration. Who else?

16:20 All the brethren send greetings. Greet one another with a holy kiss. What could be more natural than such a gesture of Christian affection? It is a "holy kiss" because it gives outward expression to the love that is the inner dynamic of "let all you do be done in love" (1 Cor 16:14). The holy kiss is the sacrament of love. But, like all holy things, it was open to abuse from the earliest times. Indeed, such abuse influenced the architecture of churches, which segregated the men from the women, and even-

tually led to the disappearance of the practice from liturgical cel-
ebrations until more recent times.

16:21 I, Paul, write this greeting with my own hand. Having,
according to his usual practice, dictated the letter to the
Corinthians, Paul now takes the pen in hand to affix his signature,
a pledge of its authenticity.

*16:22 If any one has no love for the Lord, let him be accursed
[Greek: anathema]. Our Lord, come!* Despite its appearance, this
is not a curse, but a warning. The one who "has no love for the
Lord" decrees his own condemnation and requires no external
agent to curse him.

Paul transliterates into Greek a familiar Christian petition:
marana tha, "Our Lord, come!" Nothing could be more natural to
him who expected the answer to this prayer in his own lifetime. For
a Christian believer in any age, aware of existence between the "he
ascended into heaven" and the "he shall come again" of the Creed,
"Come Lord, come!" has to be prayer's natural expression.

*16:23–24 The grace of the Lord Jesus be with you. My love be with
you all in Christ Jesus. Amen.*

FOR FURTHER READING

Barrett, C. K., *The First Epistle to the Corinthians* (Black's New Testament Commentary; Baker Academic Press 1993) 432 pages.

Bray, Gerald L. (editor), *1–2 Corinthians* (Ancient Christian Commentary on Scripture. New Testament VII; IVP Academic Press 2012) 372 pages.

Collins, Raymond, *First Corinthians* (Sacra Pagina 7; Liturgical Press 1999) 703 pages.

Fitzmyer, Joseph A., *First Corinthians* (Anchor Bible Commentary; Yale University Press 2008) 688 pages.

Furnish, Victor Paul, *The Theology of the First Letter to the Corinthians* (Cambridge University Press 1999) 188 pages.

Horsley, Richard A., *1 Corinthians* (Abingdon New Testament Commentaries; Abingdon Press 1998) 240 pages.

Montague, George T., *First Corinthians* (Catholic Commentary on Sacred Scripture; Baker Academic Press 2011) 320 pages.

Murphy-O'Connor, Jerome, *St. Paul's Corinth. Texts and Archeology* (Liturgical Press 2002) 256 pages.

Perkins, Pheme, *1 Corinthians* (Paideia Commentaries on the New Testament; Baker Academic Press 2012) 256 pages.

Witherington III, Ben, *A Week in the Life of Corinth* (IVP Academic Press 2012) 159 pages.